GOOD
AUTHORITY

HOW TO BECOME THE

LEADER

YOUR TEAM IS WAITING FOR

GOOD

AUTHORITY

JONATHAN RAYMOND

IDEAPRESS
PUBLISHING

IDEAPRESS
PUBLISHING

Published by IdeaPress Publishing, Washington DC

IDEAPRESS PUBLISHING
WE PUBLISH BRILLIANT BUSINESS BOOKS
www.ideapresspublishing.com

All trademarks are the property of their respective companies.

Cover design by Faceout Studio, Jeff Miller

ISBN: 978-1-940858-19-7   MHID: 1-940858-19-4

PROUDLY PRINTED IN THE UNITED STATES OF AMERICA

IdeaPress Books are available at a special discount for bulk purchases for
sales promotions and premiums, or for use in corporate training programs.
Special editions, including personalized covers, a custom foreword,
corporate imprints, and bonus content are also available.

For more details, email info@ideapresspublishing.com.

No animals were harmed in the writing, printing, or distribution of this book.
The trees, however, were not so lucky.

The privilege of a lifetime
is to become who you truly are.

—C.G. Jung

CONTENTS

THE GOOD AUTHORITY
MANIFESTO

GOOD AUTHORITY IS...

1.
The presence to name the things
that most people overlook

2.
The kindness to speak up today
instead of waiting until tomorrow

3.
The patience to meet each person
where they are on the journey

4.
The generosity to challenge them
to go a little bit further

5.
The fortitude to not accept excuses
in place of responsibility

6.

The curiosity to ask questions that you
don't know the answers to

7.

The wisdom to resist the comfortable answers
and hold out for the right ones

8.

The willingness to make an unpopular stand
if it helps one person grow

9.

The transparency to share what you feel
with each member of your team

10.

The strength to wait for others to discover
their own truth for themselves

11.

The integrity to never ask someone to live up
to a standard that you don't yourself

12.

The vulnerability to say what you feel even if
you think it won't change anything

13.

The audacity to assume that you can change the world

14.

And, the humility to be wrong about all of it
and start over again tomorrow

Jon Versus the Volcano

Home—is where I want to be.
But I guess I'm already there.
— **Talking Heads**

It seemed like the perfect day to hike up a volcano. But as we swallowed the last few bites of our pack-lunch the skies opened up. The gentle dirt path we'd been hiking up the last few hours was instantly transformed into a rapidly flowing river of Central American mud. We probably could've waited out the storm before heading back to the lodge. We probably should've. But we were 28 years old. So we made a run for it.

It was one of those experiences that starts out awful but becomes wonderful; awful for as long as you try and control it, wonderful when you finally let go. After a few minutes of repeated tripping and falling, I found my stride. If I lifted and stepped with just the right amount of force I could stay near the surface of the mud river, a kind of surf-walking. Pull too hard and my shoes were summarily sucked back down—and more than a few times pulled clear off—by this surprisingly sticky stuff. My traveling companions discovered it too. There was only one way to do it. And then the physical surrender turned to a mental one. My mind started to wander, freed up by the rhythmic monotony of motion. I started to feel how much pain I was actually in.

The pain was not in my legs. It was in my life. The year was 1999, and I'd graduated from law school the year before. I was one year into my first real "career"—slaving away in the bowels of a large, prestigious Manhattan law firm. I was drawn in by the money and the high stakes. When I faxed a copy of my first paycheck to my grandmother she called me a minute later to let me know it must've been a clerical error and that I should just keep quiet and hope they didn't notice.

I loved the negotiations, the intellectual challenge of organizational structure, high finance, and the opportunity to learn from people at the very top of the game. But the personal price was impossibly high. Everyone around me was miserable. There were unbearable tyrants in the corner offices. But, like every other business I've ever come across, this one was mostly filled with kind and dedicated people trying to make the best of a tough situation.

The problem was the inhumanity of it all: the unrealistic expectations of leadership; a team of people who might otherwise be friends forced to compete with each other over resources; a toxic mix of power and unconscious behavior that left people feeling like they didn't matter, that they didn't have a voice, and that the only way to survive was to put their heads down and bear it. It was a profitable business. And a human disaster area.

That law firm was an extreme workplace in one way. But, as I would come to learn over the next few decades, when it came to the things that really mattered—to the emotional world where human beings live—it was far more the norm than I ever would've imagined.

But I didn't have the life experience to know that while we were sliding down the volcano. The experience I had was far more simple: I was single, stressed-out, and depressed. And while I was no authority on souls—my family's bible was *The New York Times*—I was certain that mine was seriously adrift. Somehow, in this one moment, I realized that continuing down the road I was on was no longer an option. I had to leave. I was still young enough to not worry too much about what would happen when I did. We were halfway down the trail when the words reached my lips.

"I'm done!" I threw my head to the sky and screamed out loud into the torrential rain. My very own Shawshank moment. I continued on with my personal pep talk. "I can't spend another day pretending that this is okay. Everyone I work with is miserable. And nobody is doing anything about it. There has got to be a better way. I'm going to walk into Doug's office on Monday morning and give my two weeks' notice."

Monday morning arrived. I was back at work and it was time to put my new-found resolve to the test. Quitting meant telling the boss—the senior partner in my department and one of the "Top 100 Lawyers in New York" (yes, that's a thing). He was a small man and scary as hell. The screaming, brutish, Napoleon type. He was not what I would call a Good Authority.

I walked past his office three or four times, trying to work up the nerve, his secretary eyeing me and wondering what this was all about. Finally, I knocked on his open door. "Come on in," he said, in a friendly tone that more than a little took me by surprise. "What can I do for you?" he asked.

"I've decided to leave the firm."

And with those six little words, all of a sudden we were equals. Just two guys in a room. I wasn't afraid anymore.

"I'm not happy. I don't know what I want to do with my life, but this isn't it."

"Is there anything we can do to change your mind?" he asked with a curiosity I had never experienced with him before.

"No, there really isn't. I appreciate you asking, but it's time for me to go."

"Do you know what you're going to do?" By now I could tell that half of his mind had moved on to the next task on his list.

"I'm going to Vermont to do a week-long meditation retreat."

As he shifted in his chair I could tell that the answer made him uncomfortable. He told some bad joke to break the tension, I laughed politely and walked out. It's amazing how the authority figures we idolize crumble the moment we stop holding them up. It wasn't the last time I'd learn that lesson.

I signed up for eight days of silence. Voluntarily. I pondered the wisdom of that decision as I pulled onto I-91 for the four-hour trip north to Vermont. "Jonathan, what are you thinking?" I muttered to myself in a variety of different voices. "Go home. You don't need to do this." I managed to stay in the car. Amidst the grueling torture of that retreat—eight days with nothing but my thoughts—something happened. It wasn't enlightenment.

But it was a profound experience—an experience of myself. Not who I wanted to be. Not who I thought I should be. Nobody special. Just me—bones and flesh, thoughts and emotions coming and going. It was beautiful. Better than any drug—and I'd tried more than one. In that moment I made a decision, as much as you can decide anything long-term when you're 28, unemployed, and single. I was going to ride that self-discovery train as far as it would take me.

I spent the better part of the next decade doing just that. I had jobs and ventures to pay the bills. But my heart was in the search. I went on more and longer retreats. I travelled to high mountains in faraway places to look for wise teachers. I moved to San Francisco, which, to a Jewish kid from the New York suburbs, was the mecca for all things weird and leading edge. I helped to start a renewable energy business. I dove headlong into the world of alternative healing: studied to be a yoga teacher, trained in somatic psychotherapy, and considered going back to school to get a master's in psychology. I joined up with some friends to create a nonprofit that teaches meditation and mindfulness to kids in juvenile hall. I fell in love and had the first real long-term relationship of my life.

Along the way I found a few things that I was genuinely good at and could have made a career of. But I still couldn't shake that feeling. The one that was sure that whatever I was supposed to be doing with my life, I hadn't found it yet. It turns out, I didn't need to. It was about to find me.

In 2011 I came across an opportunity that I couldn't resist. I took on the CEO role at EMyth, the business coaching company behind the well-known book. The owner had decided to relocate the company to Ashland, Oregon, the small town halfway between Portland and San Francisco where I was living. Finding myself at the helm of a name-brand coaching company, with a mandate to revitalize the culture and take things in a new direction, was the kind of big city opportunity that I never imagined I'd find in a town known primarily for its annual Shakespeare Festival.

The first few years were a thrilling and wild ride. I was still pursuing my own personal work on the side, but the leadership journey I was on was too exciting to leave room for much else. I had a platform to express myself out in the world, the kind I'd always dreamed of. Along with my co-managers and our small but dedicated team, we took the company through a full-blown transformation: from culture and brand to technology and process, and everything in between. The team was inspired. The brand came back to life. People whose books I'd read said they loved my writing and the new message. Consultants who'd been around the corporate-transformation block praised the changes we'd made.

But there was a mismatch. It was there from the start, but I didn't notice it from the uniquely weird viewpoint that comes with the CEO title. I was managing the business in the only way I knew, fast and full of risk. But being in a small town created some very real limits. The pace and kinds of risks I wanted to take were out of step with the stability and lifestyle most people move to a small town to have. People were genuinely inspired by what we were doing, but I was leading a different company in my head than the one that was there on the ground.

Isn't it incredible how life brings you the voice you need to hear in the moment you need to hear it? I was in mid-realization of that mismatch when I went to a conference and heard two well-known corporate visionaries—Gary Hirshberg of Stonyfield Farm and Curt Richardson of OtterBox—share their stories of stepping out of the CEO role to make room for the leader the business needed next. My next step was as excruciating as it was clear: It was time for me to let go of what felt like my baby and make room for someone else. Second to meeting my wife, *stepping out of the CEO role and into a supporting one was the best thing that ever happened to me.*

Over the next two years I had two unique new experiences that few leaders ever have the "good fortune" to get. The first was that I got a taste of my own medicine. I saw what it was like to live and work in the culture that I'd created: The unrealistic pace of projects, how my appetite for risk was not shared by everyone on the team, how what looked like a clear initiative in a leadership meeting could still be incredibly confusing to the team trying to implement it. In my new business, this is one of the things we work actively with CEOs to see: how one idea from the top can spiral into 100 projects for the team and overwhelm them in ways the CEOs can't even imagine.

But the second experience was the one that really hit me. It was that, as the CEO, I was radically overestimating the quality of mentoring that most managers—myself included—were doing with the people on their team. It's a phenomenon I see repeating itself every day in the work I do now with managers at every level in different organizations around the world. What managers are doing, including some of the smartest and most caring people I've ever met, has almost no real mentoring to it. And even the mentoring they're trying to do to get people to take personal responsibility is undermined by the background company culture dynamics that send a very different message: Keep your head down, do your job, and don't rock the boat.

It's incredibly easy for the CEO to miss. Under the enormous pressure of the role, their vision gets tighter. It becomes finely tuned to fluctuations in numbers and goals, and less sensitive to the interpersonal and interdepartmental dynamics. Employees start to feel less important even though you, as the CEO, know they're not. And because you're the person who holds everyone else's paycheck in your hands, you almost never get honest feedback about how people are feeling. That is, until they're frustrated enough to quit or they act out enough to get fired.

When it comes to employee development, what managers do—what I was doing—was almost exclusively the easy stuff: encouraging words, good advice, and, more than anything, jumping in to fix short-term problems to keep projects moving along. But what my team needed was something else entirely. They needed me to listen. They needed me to hear what they were saying and do something about it. They needed me to hear what they weren't saying and use that insight to create more definition to their role so that there was even a job for them to own. And they needed me to set clear boundaries and make sure everyone was held accountable to the same standard. They were not lazy. They were not incompetent. And they were not uncaring. They were waiting.

I made a decision. Since I'd tried everything else, I was going to try something new, something that I'd written a lot of blog posts and delivered a lot of webinars and workshops about but had never really done. Not with all my heart. I was going to let my team tell me what they needed from me instead of me telling them what I needed from them. I was going to help them grow personally and trust that the professional side would take care of itself. I was going to do everything in my power—which was still quite a lot—to improve the experience of working there. I decided to do whatever I could to create a great place to work, *one conversation at a time*.

I started talking with each person on my team in a new way. I asked them far more personal questions than I'd dared to do before—not about their personal lives, but about their personal relationship to their work. I did a lot less assuming that I knew, or was supposed to know, the answers. I took the risk to let my guard down and shared more of how I struggled with some of the very same issues they did. They responded. They took ownership of their work in ways I always wanted them to but never knew how to bring out of them. And what was most rewarding for me was that the changes they were making translated into other parts of their lives. Sometimes I would hear about it directly, other times I could tell by how they talked about their lives in the water-cooler moments of the day. A few of those conversations when I got to hear it directly were what gave me the confidence to keep going.

I was in my office wrapping up a few things before heading home one afternoon. One of the guys on my team, who'd been working for me for about a year, stopped by on his way out the door. He was smart, capable, and was doing fine work. Still, as I'd come to know him over time, I had a sense that he had a whole other gear. For some reason, he was holding himself back. I'd made it my mission to find out why, and to see if I could help him take the next step in his own growth. We talked about the theme every week in our individual meetings. I gave him small assignments to push himself out of his comfort zone a bit more each week. I pointed out the micro-behaviors (more on that in Chapter Five)—the way he showed up in meetings, how he negotiated project changes with his teammates—anything I saw that felt connected to the larger theme. And I held him accountable when he slid back into his old pattern of being too agreeable, instead of speaking his mind and taking the risk to innovate when he saw a better way.

"Do you have a minute?" he said.

"Sure, come on in."

"Hey, so I don't know how to say this, but I just want to say thank you." (He wasn't someone who had an easy time talking about himself.) "I know you're busy and have a lot on your plate but you gave me something these past few months that I'll never forget—an experience of myself out in the world— that I didn't know I was missing. And it's making a big difference at home too."

"Really?" I replied. "That's so great to hear. I don't want to put you on the spot but I'd love to hear a little more about it if you're up for sharing."

"Well, my two boys just look at me differently now. I don't know what other words to use but I can see it in their eyes, I'm just more there. Do you know what I mean?"

He had done the real work of changing. He took the feedback I'd given him along the way. He broke the pattern, one moment at a time, of undermining his own creativity and entrepreneurial spirit by worrying too much about ruffling other people's feathers.

The conversation was different with each person. Sometimes it was simply having a new experience of what it was like to have a boss, someone who listened, who cared, and who genuinely wanted to help.

I kept going. Over time I forgave myself for the leadership sins of my past. I did whatever I could, with everyone I could, to hold up my end of the bargain and let them make their own choices about whether they wanted to change. I learned that a manager can foster the personal growth of each person on their team by giving direct and granular feedback about the way they relate with their work, and by giving them the choice to act—or not act—on that feedback in their own way. That's what *Good Authority* is all about.

The more I saw what was missing from my own approach the more I saw the same gap in the coaching and consulting industry that I was a part of. Everyone is talking about accountability but nobody is defining what it really means, and, more importantly, breaking it down into a set of skills that people can learn and apply. The reason nobody is teaching it is because it doesn't fit into neat boxes. It's messy. It's personal. It's about who we think we are, who we find out we are when we get into relationships with other people, and the long and winding road that it takes to close the gap between the two. This discovery was also bringing me to the end of my own long and winding road, the one I started all those years before when I left the law firm in New York. I had finally closed the gap in my life between the personal me and the professional me, which never should have been there in the first place.

When I did, that voice started stirring in me again, telling me it was time to move on. I saw the potential in those moments, in the possibility that the line we've been keeping between personal and professional growth—*the line I was keeping in myself all those years*—was not only artificial, but the very thing preventing us from creating the cultures we really want. It was time for me to take the risk, to create a platform for these ideas and see what would happen. That integration of personal and professional growth has become my life's work. It's what we teach at refound.com and it's what the rest of this book is about.

Leaving my team was hard. But in the Spring of 2015 I decided that it was time for me to go out on my own. I wondered whether I could make a business out of doing just this one thing: If I could create a new kind of consultancy, a mentoring company of sorts, to teach others to apply these ideas for themselves. With the incredible curiosity and passion of a small group of clients who were there with us at the beginning, we were off.

I wrote this book to share with you the ideas—both the philosophical framework and the tactical skills—that our clients are using to change things where they work. They are people just like you: team leaders, senior managers, and C-level executives—consultants and coaches too. In the pages to come you'll be hearing from them through stories and dialogues that will help you see how much power you have to change the world where you work, no matter where on the org chart you sit.

This is not a rulebook, and it doesn't describe a linear process. It offers a new management theory and a set of skills you can test out, and decide for yourself if they work. It's a way of leading and managing a team that applies no matter what industry you're in, no matter how big or small your team. Take the time to go in order if you can. Feel free to skip ahead and come back if one of the later chapters jumps out at you. I'll meet you in the middle.

INTRODUCTION

Good Authority

> *We teach best what we*
> *most need to learn.*
> **—Richard Bach**

When I was eleven years old I went with my mother to work for the day. Her office was a college classroom. She was a psychology professor at a local university. As fate would have it, on that particular day, the discussion turned to a question that cut to the heart of why men do the things they do. "Why is it," she asked the room full of undergraduates "that, even when they're lost, men won't ask for directions?"

The class chuckled. They gave it their best shot. Of course, I thought I had a better answer. I tightened my grip on my Aquaman lunchbox to bolster my confidence. I raised my hand and waited for her to notice. Not surprisingly, she did. "Well," I said to warm myself up, "the reason men don't ask for directions is so … that way … when they figure it out they get to be the hero." As you can imagine, I've never lived that one down.

As much mileage as it got as a family anecdote over the years, there was something else going on there. There were at least three things I see now in the naive words of that eleven-year-old boy. The first was that I was expressing a belief about authority, *about what I thought it means to be of value to others*, that would become my life's work three decades later. The second was that this phenomenon had nothing to do with gender. In the work I do every day with our clients, I see female leaders and managers struggle with it just as much as us menfolk. And the third—what was obvious to my mother and probably everyone else in the room—was that I was talking about myself.

The belief many of us have as we try to figure out what it means to truly lead a team of people is this: *What makes us valuable, what gives us authority and credibility in the eyes of others, is our ability to solve problems and reach goals.* The theory of this book is that the *opposite* is true. That the highest form of leadership, the most value you can add—to your team, your organizations, and to the world around you—is to develop the strength to not give people the answers. Rather, your job is to create a space where they can discover the answers for themselves, where you become a resource for them to reach their destination. If you make the pivot, you'll find that 90 percent of the symptoms and struggles that overwhelm your day right now will start to disappear.

That's what it means to be a Good Authority. It's about becoming a true mentor to the people on your team. And I'll argue that solving your team's problems for them is not only not the solution, it is the hidden cause of many of those problems in the first place. It's why people don't own their work. It's why they make sloppy mistakes and don't care about the customer in the ways you want. And it's why every single meeting you have ends with talking about how people need to communicate better.

Good Authority is based on three core principles that we'll be teasing out and developing along the way. As you embark on the rest of this journey, keep them in mind. Let them work on you. If you're anything like me, they can be a source of growth to you for years to come, helping you re-evaluate old assumptions about what it means to lead, about the purpose of work, and giving you permission to challenge people to go beyond where they are today.

1. The deepest purpose of a business is to change the lives of the people who work there.

2. The role of leaders and managers is to show people how professional and personal growth are inseparable.

3. The way to get people to be engaged is to be more engaged with them.

Now a few words about what *Good Authority* is not. This is not a book about achieving great wealth or tripling your sales this quarter—though I'll be the first to congratulate you if you do. It's not a substitute for the many other things you can do to humanize your business, like improving benefits packages, offering more flexible hours and remote work options, and so on. It's a call to invest in a process that speaks to a different level: to our experience of work itself. To go all in with each person on your team. To discover who they are, what they're about, and how you can help them grow.

Before we move on, we need to reframe the question the coaching and consulting industry has taught business leaders to ask. The right question isn't "How do I get my people to engage?" The right question is: "How can I get better at engaging with them?"

This book is for anyone with a passion to change the status quo, anyone who believes that the world—your world—can be better than it is. It's for leaders and managers in any industry, for-profit business, or not-for-profit business. Above all, it's for anyone who has the awesome responsibility of having authority over another human being's paycheck. This is a book about caring—for the heart, spirit, and financial future of the people in your charge.

What you'll find throughout are methods and tools to help you have a new kind of conversation with each person on your team. I encourage you to use the tools as you see fit, to trust yourself, to make mistakes and learn. It isn't magic, though I hope it sometimes feels that way. It won't turn everyone on your team into a perfect team player overnight. You may get it wrong more times than you get it right. But if you invest in the journey, if you seek out feedback on how you're doing from people you trust, and keep working at it, something amazing can happen to you.

Here's a short overview of what you'll find from here on out. In Part One—**Why Should I Care?**—we'll take a fresh look at the company culture problem. We'll confront the most common myths about employee engagement, offer a new way to think about strengths and weaknesses, and close with a new vision for how everyone can share in the transformation instead of waiting for it to happen from the top down.

In Part Two—**Personal Growth at Work**—we'll attempt to bridge the gap between the personal growth revolution that's exploded over the last half-century and our current management theories that are bogged down by obsolete ideas about human motivation. We'll offer a new method for creating a culture of accountability that helps people grow at work and in life at the same time.

And in Part Three—**More Yoda, Less Superman**—we'll focus in on the specific tools and strategies you can use to develop your mentoring skills, including a new leadership archetype system in "Fixer, Fighter, or Friend?," as well as a new perspective on how to draw out each person's individual strengths in "The Five Employee Archetypes."

You'll quickly see that this book isn't really a business book. It's a book about relationships, about bringing the best of who we are to work, and slowing down the moments that matter. It's about changing the world—starting with the people just down the hall.

PART I

WHY SHOULD I CARE?

CHAPTER ONE

WHY SHOULD I CARE?

> *You're only as young as the last time
> you changed your mind.*
> —Timothy Leary

I like cleaning the kitchen. I don't love it—it'd be nice if the kitchen would clean itself every once in awhile—but I like it. The more time I spend looking at screens and living in our digital world, the more satisfaction I get from the analog side of life. My daughter, on the other hand, has not yet discovered the joys of household cleaning. In fairness, she's only eleven.

Nevertheless, my wife and I are slowly but surely giving her more responsibility around the house. She's a slippery student though. Her delay tactics are many and wondrous—the "I'm hungry," the innocent doe eyes, and when all else fails, "Well I have to do my homework first, right?" We started as you'd expect, explaining why doing her chores was important, and describing the values we were trying to instill in her. We issued our share of gentle and not-so-subtle reminders. We tried to raise the stakes with all the typical parenting bribes—a little more or less allowance, a little more or less screen time. But it didn't catch. No matter what tactics we used to try to cause the problem to go away, it didn't. We dropped the subject for a while. The stakes weren't all that high. It's not that we weren't frustrated, but she's a great kid and the process had us all laughing more than anything else. And then it happened.

It was early evening on a weeknight. I was in my home office wrapping up my day when my wife peeked in. "Follow me," she said, with a stealthy wave of her hand. We walked quietly down the stairs and turned the corner to get a view into the kitchen. And there she was. Our daughter, moving gracefully around the kitchen, sponge in hand, dish towel on her shoulder … she was cleaning … and humming her favorite song. I may have cried.

Isn't it amazing how simple and beautiful it is when someone owns their work? How in an instant, the conflict between the self-interest of "the worker" and the self-interest of "the boss" just disappears? And isn't it strange how rare an occurrence that is in our world? So, being a pest—and being in the middle of writing a book about authority—I had to know why. But I also knew that my wife, the person who's taught me the most about what inhabiting authority with grace looks like, was the right person to ask her. Turns out, it all started with cleaning her room.

Or, better said, with not cleaning her room. And then one day, she was sitting and reading on the comfy chair in the corner of our bedroom (which was clean, thank you very much) and something hit her. "It just feels better in here," she thought. "My room is so cluttered, so much stuff lying around. It's hard to find the things I want. In here I just feel more calm." In the hour before we discovered her in the kitchen, this is what she'd been doing: organizing her room—including what I can assure you is the world's most ecologically diverse collection of stuffed animals—cleaning off her desk, and stacking her clothes neatly in her closet.

From a psychological perspective, you might see her behavior as the emergence of self-care, or maybe self-authority, or perhaps self-esteem. But as her parents, it was pure joy. She knew it was what we wanted her to do but she had discovered her own reasons for doing it. And she had discovered the best reason, the one that trumps all others: She did it because she liked the way it made her feel.

Is there anything more you could want for the people on your team?

She's not our employee. But we are the central authority figures in her life. We tried carrots and sticks, the parenting variety, and that didn't work. What worked was creating the space for her to own it for herself. One of the ingredients in creating that space was not cleaning up her world for her. Have you ever been given a gift like that from someone you worked for—the gift of them not jumping in and saving you, so you had no choice but to figure it out for yourself? The other ingredient was keeping our world clean. Have you ever worked for someone like that, someone who truly embodied their values, and didn't say one thing and do another when doing the right thing was hard?

Change was not caused by what we said or how many

times we said it. She didn't start cleaning because we shared a bold vision for cleanliness, or a family-wide goal of a certain number of socks per week in the hamper. It didn't come from a better explanation of the problem, a clearer process, or checking in with her to see how it was going! The source of change was contrast, her personal experience of a gap: the pain of feeling where she was compared to where she wanted to be.

Isn't that outcome what we're spending billions of dollars, and countless hours, trying to create at work? We go to leadership workshops to figure out how to inspire and create clearer visions. We send our people to management trainings to help them learn to prioritize and get better at positive reinforcement, motivations, and incentives. We drag people to cheesy team-building workshops to create a feeling of common interest. We buy ping-pong tables and catered lunches to try and make it fun. We try our hand at the power of positive thinking, the secret to manifesting success.

We devour leadership and self-help books. We learn inspiring new ideas. Hope is restored. We create systems, clarify policies, write and rewrite our values statements, try to discover our "Why?" and encourage our people to do the same. But no matter what we try, no matter how well-intentioned, no matter how smart or well-educated the leaders of the organization, the problem persists. We still find ourselves flailing around, looking for the magic key that will reach people where they live. We keep asking over and over again, "How can I get people to own their work?" We get no answer.

That doesn't mean that nothing happens. Carrots and sticks,

including the New Age variety, work to an extent. The dangling of promotions, the promise of raises and bonuses, chair massages, and yoga classes, all can elicit a general sense of compliance, more or less. We still reach goals. We get hard work—which is not the same as great work. But these tactics don't give you what you really want. What you want is a feeling—the same feeling that every leader who has ever lived craves: "They've got this. I can relax."

Why don't any of these tactics get us to that place? It's because they all have something in common. Can you see it?

It's that they all start with the needs of the business, and put the needs of the individuals second, usually a distant second.

This orientation—this worldview that transcends any management theory—rests on a pillar that goes back to the Industrial Revolution. It says "The company has a goal. The people are here as a resource to do whatever the machines cannot, to reach that goal." Hence the Orwellian term that lives on to this day: human resources. It follows from this that the job of authority, of all the layers of management, is to extract what they need from the people. At the heart of this approach to business is a subtle but powerful idea, one that we still haven't shaken more than two centuries later: Work is for the boss.

But times changed. People started waking up to their options. The small business revolution that started in the 1970s and is still gaining speed began to cause a problem for the more established businesses. All of a sudden, their best people had an option that was more appealing and more realistic than ever before. It was still incredibly risky, but when people are feeling taken advantage of, the risk factor has a funny way of seeming a whole lot lower than it actually is.

The business world noticed. CEOs, leaders and managers, consultants and coaches, are not stupid people. They knew something had to be done. The company culture movement was born. And as this book is going to press, this industry is on fire. It seems there's another company launched every day, including my own, to try and solve the latest version of the same problem: How do I attract and retain a team of talented people?

The voices of "what to do about it" come in different flavors. Some focus more on the compensation side of things, the direct and indirect financial perks and benefits. Others focus on increasing the "fun factor," through culture activities and team-building exercises. The relative new kids on the block encourage owners to bring their personal and spiritual values into the office—we see business leaders talking about approaches based in mindfulness, conscious communication, and other forms of personal growth, and offering their staff opportunities to practice them on company time. There's so much good intention in the mix, so many people trying to change things for the better.

But the numbers on engagement and culture are still as bad as they ever were and getting worse. Because all of the solutions you're being offered—well-intentioned as they are—are asking you put a layer on top of the authority problem, to solve it by not solving it, as it were. That might have worked forty years ago, or twenty, or even five. Not anymore. Carrots and sticks, even the most sophisticated, spiritually wise, and compassionate-sounding ones you can find, will be spotted from a mile away. Millennials were seemingly born with this X-ray vision, but everyone has it now. We need to know "Why?" And the answer had better be good. People who have a choice will no longer work to serve your reasons, your goals. They will not work to serve your authority, they will only work to serve their own. Not because you're a mean person. But because in our modern world, even people who are living paycheck to paycheck—which is just about everybody—are rising up and saying "No." They're saying, "I have a choice. I want something more than this. I don't know what it is, but I'm going to keep looking until I find it."

What does that mean for you, the modern leader? It means you have to offer something they can't get on their own, a perk that transcends all others, a perk that has nothing to do with the business. It's the offer of work that will—from the the day they start to the day they decide to move on—help them become a better version of themselves. It's the promise that you will use your authority to help them discover theirs. It's, in a fundamental way, learning to speak a new language. The language of self-authority. How do you learn that language for yourself? How do you help the people on your team gain fluency? What keeps you from speaking it today? Now those are a bunch of questions worth answering.

CHAPTER TWO

BORROWED AUTHORITY

When you make your peace with authority,
you become authority.
—Jim Morrison

We have good reason to mistrust authority—some of us more than others. We've been betrayed. We've been misled, sold one thing and delivered another, over and over. We've been manipulated, taken advantage of. We've been abused—sometimes subtly, sometimes not. You have all the experience a person needs to make a reasonable conclusion: authority is the problem. It's reasonable but it's not true. The problem is not authority, it's that we haven't learned how to inhabit authority in a way that's truly coming from our own heart and conscience.

The opposite of Good Authority isn't Bad Authority—it's Borrowed Authority. Borrowed in the sense that the authority is not our own. It's the one we learned—from our parents, from our culture, from our teachers. And, for the purposes of this book, authority also consists of the strategies and tactics we've learned from the coaches, management consultants, and gurus who have promised us that they have the answer. There's only one authority we haven't tried, though it takes a lifetime to discover: our own.

I was working with the owner of a small technology company. In his early 50s, Mike was the picture of kind leadership. He was skilled in his craft, quick with a smile. He cared about the lives of the people on the team and had the drive of a man who knew that the world makes no promises. There was only one problem—his business had been stuck in neutral for the better part of a decade. No matter what he tried, he couldn't get people to own their work. He wasn't attracting a next generation of leaders, people who would carry the business beyond where he could on his own. The symptom, the day-to-day form that all of this took, was a lack of accountability across the organization.

One day, on a video call with half a dozen business owners I was working with at the time, we got into a conversation about authority—Mike's. After a minute or two—I've never been able to play the part of the patient, "wait for it to organically arise" coach—I asked him a question. "Mike, what's your greatest fear when it comes to authority?" (And, Mr. President, I have a follow-up question.) He pondered for a few moments and a knowing smile washed across his face. "I don't know if this is what you're asking, but I have a thought that comes to mind."

"Oh, really … what is it?" You could hear the other six people on the call breathing.

"What I'm thinking about is my father. You see, he was an engineer—pretty high up in his firm but not the boss. My whole childhood all I heard about was how the higher-ups were screwing people, this, that, or the other way."

"How do you think that informs the way you lead the team now?"

"Oh, it's obvious now that you ask … everything I do is to not be that kind of authority."

Without ever intending to, Mike had invented an antidote. In order to not be that kind of authority, he took on one of the three leadership archetypes that you'll learn more about in Chapter Twelve, "Fixer, Fighter, or Friend." He had taken on the role of the friend. The problem was that Mike's cure, like each one of them, had serious, viral side effects. Your team can't treat you as a friend and the boss at the same time.

Mike started to make the connections. He started to see that he had a real problem. In order to step into the role that his team needed—to be willing to be tough when tough was called for—he had to discover a kind of leadership that his father's influence kept him from being able to see. He had to open himself up to a kind of tough that wasn't cruel, as his father's bosses were, but was simply firm and clear in its boundaries. In other words, Mike had to let go of the picture of authority that he had borrowed from his father.

The irony was that Mike couldn't be that kind of authority—the kind of authority his father was so disgusted by—even if he tried. His style, the man he'd become over his many years as an employee before breaking out on his own, was one of personal warmth and curiosity. He knew what it was like to work for someone else, and erred, often to a fault, on the side of giving people the benefit of the doubt.

Over the next few months Mike took up this new challenge. He started showing up with some more toughness. Not tough as in harsh, but tough as in firm. He stopped being available at all hours on his cell phone. He stopped replying on group emails that his manager should be handling. He had tough conversations with each person on the team about what personal responsibility looks like in practice, using examples from things that had happened that day. He started embodying accountability instead of talking about it. He required others to think, do, and adapt without his oversight, at every chance he could find.

This was anything but a cakewalk for Mike. He would show up on our call week after week and report on how it was going. Like all real change, his was often a case of two steps forward, one step back. But, at some point, he crossed a threshold. The team realized that the new Mike was there to stay. This wasn't a cakewalk for them, either. It wasn't as comfortable to work there anymore. When you've been working for someone for a long time, you get used to their style. Out of self-preservation, you quickly learn what riles them up and what calms them down. You use your strengths to compensate for their weaknesses. The team had to re-learn how to operate with the New Mike, and they didn't always like it. But when we talked with them (which is part of our approach, we don't work with CEOs without working with their team), we started hearing about how they appreciated having clarity and knowing where they stood. And they reported a feeling they hadn't had in a while: inspiration. They looked forward to coming to work with a sense that the business was going somewhere again. And Mike hadn't uttered one word of theory or made one big speech. He just stopped being the guy who was afraid of the past.

And, as Mike found out, when you change your leadership style, disrupting these long-held patterns of authority, the people on your team will be confused for a while. However, in my experience, most people will also see the upside and use it as an opportunity for growth, because you're finally alleviating the burden they've been living with for a long time. And then there will likely be a few people on your team who, for whatever reason, are at a place in their lives where they are looking for stability and not growth, with its more dramatic ups and downs. They will be more reluctant to make the pivot. The key is to remember something you've probably already experienced multiple times in your career: When someone on the team discovers that where they are is not the right place for them, and decides to move on, it ends up being a win for everyone.

What Mike had been doing, until he started changing it, was what we all do in one form or another. It's human. It's natural. It's reasonable. As children, and for all the years of our lives until and even after we find ourselves in a position of authority in our career, we rely on the authority stories that we internalized in the formative moments of our lives. The task of becoming a Good Authority is to find these stories, to understand how and why they got there, to respect the truth and lessons they contain—and then to let them go.

That's the journey. It's a journey that leads to a profound new space that is less cluttered by the pictures of the past—where you can listen to the people on your team in a new way. When you clear out your own baggage around authority—which is what Part II is all about—you will automatically start noticing that baggage in others. You'll start to see it and hear it and be able to help people discover how the things they're struggling with—accountability in themselves and others, taking creative risks and drawing that out of others, focusing on the important details and being able to train that in others—are all sourced in the most important management tool there is: the human heart.

CHAPTER THREE

THE EMPLOYEE ENGAGEMENT FALLACY

*People are people, so why should it be
you and I should get along so awfully?*
—Depeche Mode

The road to a disengaged team is paved with good intentions. Nobody sets out to make their employees overwhelmed, stressed-out, and miserable. Well, I suppose there are a few people like that out there. But, by and large, and as hard as it may be to accept, if you get to know even the most horrible boss you've ever met, there's a good-hearted person in there, someone who cares about the well-being of others. The problem is they have internalized a set of powerful unconscious ideas about: (1) why people don't do what they ask, and (2) what tools they have at their disposal to change things. I call this pair of ideas the Employee Engagement Fallacy.

Forbes contributor Kevin Kruse defines employee engagement as: "the emotional commitment an employee has to the organization and its goals." The abysmal numbers you'll find in magazines and newspapers demonstrate the effects of the Employee Engagement Fallacy. According to Gallup, seven out of every ten workers is either disengaged or actively undermining the efforts of their organization. Yes, you read that right. You've probably also read countless articles, blog posts, and books filled with tactics to change that. But what you haven't read about—what's shockingly absent from the discussion—is tracking the other side of the relationship. What about manager engagement?

In other words, the Employee Engagement Fallacy is assuming that the lack of engagement is the employee's fault. That there's something missing over there in worker-land. Without taking employees off the hook for personal responsibility, isn't it odd that we put the onus on the person on the vulnerable side of the power dynamic? The solution lies in turning that around: In order for your employees to engage, they need to have somebody who is engaging with them.

Where did this strange and obviously unproductive fallacy come from? You didn't learn it in school. It's not in any corporate training manual I've ever seen. It's a belief that you picked up along the way without ever intending to, an idea that comes from a time before people knew what we now know about meaning, motivation, and what people are looking for from their professional lives. This false belief expresses itself in what I call The Five Employee Engagement Myths, each one of which is well past its expiration date:

1. "I can't find good people."

2. "Nobody cares as much as I do."

3. "I can't afford to invest time in someone who is just going to leave anyway."

4. "I'm not a therapist, I don't have the skills to help them with their personal problems."

5. "We just need better systems and more communication."

Not only are all these myths untrue, but turning them around is the lynchpin of changing the way you manage, lead, and, in the process, change the lives of the people around you. Let's relegate these myths to the past so we can embark on the rest of our journey with clarity and purpose.

MYTH #1:

"I can't find good people."

You meet good people all the time. You've interviewed and hired them. You brought them onto your team, excited and hopeful about the personal qualities and skills you thought they could add. And then something happened after they started working for you. What was it? How did they go from being an exciting new hire to a consistent source of frustration?

What's probably true—not always but far more than we admit to ourselves—is that you didn't invest in that good person when they arrived. You didn't give them the training they needed, or challenge them on the behaviors you noticed that you wished they would change. You didn't show them what the DNA of your business is through specific examples, so they could get a personal experience of what you mean by *care* and why they should care in that way too. Most importantly, you didn't hold them accountable in small increments along the way to give them boundaries around what needed to change and by when.

This doesn't make you an evil person, and you shouldn't use it as an opportunity to put this book down and punish yourself for all the mistakes you've ever made. Let's not do that. I invite you instead to be honest and real with how it's been, so you can change it. You picked this book up to stop managing people the way you've been doing. Sobriety is step one.

When it comes to that very personal kind of manager engagement, we are all B players. Every leader I've ever met, this author included, has a huge blind spot in this area, and we all have the same one, though it comes in different forms: It's not being able to see how, by the very act of showing up the way we do, we disempower the people around us. That is, until we learn how to get out of the way.

When you think about it, you start to see that there's no such thing as an A player. There are certainly people who have more talent than others, an extraordinary skill or specialization. But have you ever met someone like that who didn't have an equally, if not larger, shadow aspect to working with them that was related to that strength? The first thing we have to do is recognize that we ourselves are not A players. We all have something that we're working on, something inside of ourselves that makes us feel incompetent, unconfident, insecure, or all of the above. And until we deal with our own internal world—not by fixing it but by being honest with ourselves and others about it—our strength will forever be used to perpetuate the false belief about our own authority that we started with: that other people value us for what we know and how many problems we can solve.

When you start accepting the B player in yourself, you'll stop looking at employees as being not good enough. You'll start realizing that, no matter how skilled someone is, when they come in that door, into your unique business, they are a B player. They don't understand your brand, they don't know the way you do it there, they don't know how to play with the people on your team, and they certainly don't know how to work with you. It's your job to roll up your sleeves and work with them on whatever in them needs working on. For most people this work will help them do great things. Some people won't make the pivot and they'll leave or you'll have to let them go. But great management and mentoring starts with an open mind and an open heart.

MYTH #2:

"Nobody cares as much as I do."

It may be true that nobody cares about the things you care about as much as you do. But it's not true—or fair, or helpful—to think that nobody cares as much as you. They care about different things, things that matter to them, things that inspire and move them. Your job is to get the things you care about and the things they care about to match up in a way where everybody wins.

So what are the things that employees care about? What if, in the larger sense, they *are* the exact same things you care about: creative freedom, personal meaning, doing work they love, and making enough money to support their families?

As we look across the management/employee divide, it's easy to see the people on the other side as being made of different stuff than we are. They're not. They're just at a different stage, have a different appetite for risk, perhaps. And for whatever reason, they've decided to hitch their meaning wagon to yours. It's your responsibility to discover just how much they care, in ways and about things that you don't. Talk about a win/win scenario.

MYTH #3:

"I can't afford to invest time in someone who is just going to leave anyway."

Think about the person on your team who's having the most trouble right now. Okay, now do a little math as to how much time you are already investing in them. Add up all the times you've had to finish off their work that wasn't quite there, or remind them about this, that, or the other thing. Please include the nightly conversations you're having with your spouse, the complaint sessions you're having with your colleagues, and the amount of time you lie awake at night in utter frustration that they did that thing again. How many extra hours did you spend with them over the past month? Five? Ten? Too many to count? How about over the course of the last year? Now add the value of the time that you could have been spending doing the work you were supposed to be doing. If you were to add it up, you'd probably realize you've spent 100 hours of your time on this person already. And if you look at what you've been doing during that time, you'll see that it's mostly not been mentoring or development: It's been supervision. Yikes, that's ugly stuff. That word should give you chills! Supervision is what children need so they don't stick their finger in a socket. Not a good model for building a company culture for adults.

What if instead of the next 100 hours of supervision, you spend 10 hours having direct conversations with this team member about what's been going wrong, what your standards are, why they should care, how you're going to help them grow, and how you're going to hold them accountable for their growth. Don't you feel better already?

Think about it another way. Isn't *not* investing in them the surest way that they will leave—or stay and drag other people down? Think of all the good things that will happen when you train and invest in one person. Think of what it will mean to them as a human being. Think of what it will mean to you to be the kind of human being who helps other human beings with hard things. Think about the message it sends to the other people on the team that you're willing to take that kind of a risk. Think about the people below that person on the org chart who will benefit from their growth even if/when that person does leave. There's no end to the potential benefits of investing in your employees, but ultimately the most important benefit is this: It's the right thing to do.

MYTH #4:

"I'm not a therapist, I don't have the skills to help them with their personal problems."

How many things have you tried to help you become a better leader, manager, and all-around effective person? How many consultants and coaches, how many self-improvement books, podcasts, and weekend workshops? How many of those ideas have you tried to introduce into your company culture? If you're reading this, chances are you decided long ago that who you are and how you relate with your work is highly relevant to the business—and that your personal transformation would be good not just for you but for the people around you. Why doesn't the same hold true for everyone else in your business?

Even if you're ready to acknowledge that your employees' personal growth is relevant and will be good for your business, there's still this challenge: How do you broach the subject? And how do you have this more personal conversation without going beyond the bounds of the professional agreement between a manager and an employee? We'll be answering these questions throughout the rest of this book by offering many simple methods to talk about performance issues in a way that intersects beautifully with personal growth challenges. That it's hard doesn't put it off limits. It just means it's hard. And as I hope you'll discover in the rest of this book, you may be making it far harder than it needs to be.

MYTH #5:

"We just need better systems and more communication."

Systems, processes, action plans, and procedures are wonderful things. They are necessary in creating a minimum amount of order and predictability to your business. But ask yourself: How many systems do you have right now? How many hard and so-called soft documents have you written over the years with big promises as to what they were going to deliver? Vision documents, brand positions, marketing strategies, values presentations. Have any of them, honestly, done even a bit to get people to take real ownership of their work?

Systems are not the solution to people problems. They're absolutely the answer to systems problems though! The key is to know the difference. When an athlete breaks their leg you put it in a cast to help restore structure and stability. But to support them through the emotions of the fall and help them to get back up again? For that you need a whole other kind of medicine.

Let's make a new set of operating assumptions. They're not the opposite of the myths we've hopefully just debunked, but a reframe that allows us to approach the growth conversation with the honesty and nuance that we all deserve:

"I can't find good people" becomes "I can't know who my A players are until I challenge them to find out."

"Nobody cares as much as I do" becomes "I haven't figured out how they care in their own way that can harmonize with the way that I do."

"I can't afford to invest time in someone who is just going to leave anyway" becomes "I don't have time to do anything else."

"I'm not a therapist, I don't have the skills to help them with their personal problems" becomes "I'm not a therapist, but I am two steps ahead of this person as a professional and can help them grow by sharing the things I've learned along the way."

"We just need better systems and more communication" becomes "We don't need more communication. We need to start speaking a different language."

Imagine for a moment that you were to start living into these new assumptions bit by bit, a little more each day. Who do you want to go and talk to first?

CHAPTER FOUR

From Strength to Growth

Most people spend their whole lives using their strengths to cover up and hide their weaknesses. But, if you surrender to your weakness, therein lies your pathway to genius.

—Moshe Feldenkrais

Cheryl had a knack for social media, an invaluable skill-set for a modern marketing team. She was a natural at coming up with new initiatives and seeing patterns in the results so we could adjust strategy. But Cheryl was not a good teammate. She was constantly pushing deadlines, increasing the scope of projects at the last minute, and she tended to dominate team meetings with her ideas, which shut down others in the process. She wasn't mean about it, the team generally respected her and looked to her for guidance. But the grumblings were there. People dropped hints to her about the way they felt bullied into agreeing with her. Cheryl wasn't picking up on the hints.

I wasn't either. Team members would complain in off-hand comments here and there. It was nothing blatant, but a little bit of having to cover for her here, a little bit of extra work because of her there. It didn't seem like that big a deal. Of course, I see now, it was very much a big deal. But I wasn't listening. If I had been, I would have done something. I even remember thinking things like, "What can I really do? I'm not her therapist, I'm her boss. And who will pick up the slack if she gets upset and walks out? Anyway, let's see what happens, if it comes up again I'll talk to her." Can you spot a few of the the Employee Engagement Myths in action? All of them?

Somewhere around that time I started waking up to a similar theme in my own life. It turned out that when it came to blind spots, Cheryl and I had more than a little bit in common. I was ten years older, we'd come from entirely different backgrounds, but in the thing that mattered—in our relationship to our work—we were birds of a feather. As long as I remained blissfully ignorant of my version of the blind spot, I couldn't help her with hers. I literally couldn't see it—they're not called blind spots by accident.

It was then that I had my window. The quiet grumblings had turned into two identical flare-ups within a matter of days. Twice Cheryl had failed to communicate scope changes to her teammates, and each time they'd had to spend an extra two days re-working something they had already crossed off their list. The grumblings bubbled over when her behavior started screwing with with her teammates' day, making it harder for them to do their work, and I had a steady stream of people coming by my office to let me know about it.

It's worth a brief detour for a moment. A great thing to do is to take a kind of personality inventory of your team. You don't need any fancy diagnostic tool. Just look around. Go by what you know of them. Who is like you? Who has a style that is more like the opposite of yours? You may be surprised to discover how likely it is that you're able to put everyone on your team into one of those two categories. As a leader, you'll tend, whether you realize you're doing it or not, to draw two kinds of people to your teams: those who are like you, because it'll be easy for you to relate with each other; and those who are diametrically unlike you, because they'll be able to fill in gaps created by your style.

As I'm sure you've already concluded, this book would caution you strongly against the wisdom of that approach— that is, trying to make up for your weaknesses through other people. But not for the reason you might think. It's not because there's no merit to that line of thinking, or because you should focus on your weaknesses instead. It's because thinking about it in linear terms of strengths/weaknesses is far too simplistic for human beings. Sometimes our greatest strength is also our greatest weakness. And what's more true, in my experience, is that the strongest people you'll ever meet are the ones who've made peace with their weaknesses—our central topic for Part III.

This dynamic—the interplay between strengths and weaknesses—was causing problems for Cheryl's teammates. Not to mention for me. There was only one person who wasn't feeling the impact: Cheryl. This is how I was failing her as her manager. I wasn't helping her make the connections. I was too willing to benefit from her strengths, too reluctant to see the impacts of her not knowing how to use them in a collaborative way. And those impacts took the form that they take for all of us: the micro-behaviors that drive the people around us crazy.

Those micro-behaviors—the communication gaffes, the time-management oversights, the budget overruns—are the liquid gold great mentors are looking for. Why are they so valuable? Not because they're opportunities to shame or punish people, but because they are doorways to conversations about the things that matter. They work as entry points because they're concrete, because there's no denying their existence, and because, to borrow a marketing term, you can back them up with social proof. Here's how the conversation between Cheryl and me played out:

"So, Cheryl," I began in a side moment one afternoon. "Did you sense anything strange about today's meeting?"

"No, I didn't. I'm really excited about this new campaign though. It's great, right?"

"It is great, I'm curious to see how people respond. But I want to focus on this morning's staff meeting for a moment." (This was the meeting where those flare-ups started that resulted in the stream of people in my office.) "Do you feel like it went well? Did you notice any tension when we were talking about the project schedule?"

After a moment of hesitation, I could see the color coming back into her face, realizing she wasn't in trouble and that I was genuinely trying to help. She was sharp, so it only took a second for her to connect the dots. She owned up to what happened, though I had to turn the screws a bit to get there, but we now had something to work with. We were talking about the same thing, the same facts. We were in the same reality, which, no matter how tense it gets, is the only way any two people ever worked out their differences—including a genuine agreement to disagree and/or part ways.

Over the next few months we went on a manager/employee journey, the kind you'll be learning about in various ways throughout this book. It wasn't strictly linear, but I made sure we spent enough time at the beginning defining the problem. I gave her an assignment to write down the specific problem behaviors and their impacts. That was the content. Then we talked about the context, what the underlying dynamics were that contributed to the problem. She shared with me some of her frustration about others' behavior, which, so long as she wasn't using that as a way to avoid responsibility for her stuff, was completely fine. We talked about some of the challenges between departments and across the company. I listened to her perspective on how we, at the leadership level, weren't fully appreciating how overwhelmed the team was. And then we made a plan, and an agreement, for what she was committed to changing, what I was committing to help her with from my side, and the timeline for the change that I was expecting from her.

I want to focus on my side—the manager's side—of the commitment: I was not going to entertain any new initiatives from Cheryl if at any point I was hearing from her colleagues or picking up on my own that her patterns weren't changing. I, of course, didn't tell any of this to her teammates—this was Cheryl's journey. And I made clear that it was her responsibility, not mine, to check in with me on how it was going and ask for whatever help she needed.

Over the next few weeks, working with Cheryl on these issues was a Post-it note in my mind. In order to help her, I went out of my way to point out the most granular details I could find: an email from me she hadn't answered within 24 hours (our team standard), a project status update she had not made before a standing meeting (per team rules), a weekly meeting with me that she arrived late to—even by five minutes—without pinging me to let me know. Like my boxing coach who won't let me stop punching until I'm coming from my legs in precisely the right way, I made it my business to sweat the smallest of stuff with Cheryl, because I knew it would help her. Because I knew it would help the team. Because her changing this pattern would be a win for everyone.

Our weekly meetings were equally intense. There was no small talk. She was in training mode. If you ever try it, you'll discover something counterintuitive: As long as it's done with kindness, and you're doing it for your own reasons and not to please your boss, being held accountable by your manager can be fun. It can liven up the day. Cut through the noise, clutter, and monotony that is a real part of life in a modern office. Topics covered in the meetings included: what steps she was taking throughout the day to challenge her old behaviors, how many times she caught herself doing that thing that she was trying to stop doing, what else she was learning, and whether there was any way I could be of more help.

Personal growth, like all real change, requires tension. The same way that creating a new vision for a business gives you an ongoing reference point for what's still old and needs to be upgraded, the new way we want to be has to bump up against the old way. The gap is what drives us, inspires us to keep finding our edge, to get feedback from people we trust about what's changing and what still needs work. It's in this process of toggling between the old and the new, of trying and failing and trying again, that we learn. And after a certain amount of time, and the application of the productive tension we're talking about here, something happens. The amount of time is likely to be longer and the process less linear than we wish, but we eventually discover a doorway we didn't see before. Pain, necessary as it was, is replaced by joy.

About a month into the process, Cheryl came bounding into my office. She had discovered what was behind her trouble at work, the story she was telling herself about her value, the pattern that was hiding until she found it, which was driving all the micro-behaviors she had been working so hard to stop. As I've found each and every time I've worked with someone on a pattern like this, the answer came to her in a surprising form.

"I've always seen my value as being the one who comes up with new ideas, in being creative," she began. "And the more I focused on the little stuff, the deadlines and all that you've been on me about, the more I felt lost, like, this can't be the point. What is my value here if I'm not out there doing more of the stuff I'm good at? And then the strangest thing happened. You know that campaign I've been working with Greg and Anne on? They did it on their own! And the idea they came up with for it is so cool. I don't get it. I mean, I get it … but I don't get it."

Cheryl was a mid-level manager, but she was describing the exact same moment I've heard from CEOs and VPs who've had their own breakthrough like that. We've distilled it down to a bit of marketing copy that you'll find on our website. We call it "More Yoda, Less Superman." It's the counterintuitive leadership pivot that comes from pulling back the version of us that knows how to save the day, and allowing a slower, quieter version to come forward. The version who asks questions, waits for other people to find the answers, and isn't it afraid to have a little fun in the process.

Cheryl went in a fairly straight line from there. The path is usually a little bumpier in my experience. But the more she focused on deadlines, on details, and on proactively communicating with others about what was on her plate, the more they responded. The conflicts and tension from the past were forgiven. The rest of the team started to listen to her again. They began to look to her for guidance again, but in a new way. They weren't seeing her as the one to go to who could get it done. They saw her as a leader. I promoted her to a new role a short while later, giving her a title that better suited the strategic focus that she was increasingly freed up to have. Her transformation didn't go in a perfectly straight line, but nobody's ever does. As time went on, particularly when she was taking on new tasks that were out of her comfort zone, she'd slip into the old pattern. But we'd talk about it and move on.

Cheryl did not become a leader in her department by doubling down on her strengths. She did it by putting those strengths on ice for a while, until she no longer needed them to cover up that feeling, until they were no longer a Band-Aid over her insecurities about her value as a worker and a person. She got there by focusing not just on the little stuff, but on a certain kind of little stuff: the micro-behaviors that impacted her teammates—including her boss—in ways that pushed us away from her. As a result, our team became closer than it ever had been.

CHAPTER FIVE

Sweat The Small Stuff

*Not knowing how near the truth is,
we seek it far away.*

– Hakuin

I'm not a good surfer. I strongly prefer a gentle two-foot slow roller to the oh-no-that-is-going-to-crash-on-my-head variety. But in my second week of learning back in 2006 I had a bit of beginner's luck. I paddled out into the water with a friend who *was* an experienced surfer, encountered some unusually big waves, and somehow found myself in the groove. Only when we got out of the water did my surfer friend tell me how very not-beginner those waves were. Luckily, I was too green to know how out of my depth I was. That's how it was with my mentoring of Cheryl too, a solid bit of Good Authority beginner's luck.

In the years that followed, I started to develop a method that brought some clarity and repeatability to the types of conversations I had with Cheryl. At Refound we've turned that method into a process that we call The Accountability Dial (which you'll learn more about in Chapter Nine) that breaks down the internal architecture of the conversations I was having with Cheryl. The Accountability Dial will show you step by step how to have these conversations with the people on your team so you don't feel like you're flying by the seat of your pants.

Accountability is a skill. And just like surfing, at least for me, it's a completely unnatural one! In surfing, there's a complex combination of things you have to consider before you paddle into a wave: the subtle shifts in the angle and peak of this wave compared to the one just before, its size and speed, the wind, your energy level, even the surfer's etiquette around where you are in the line-up and who's next. In all of this, there's one thing you have to do that's not negotiable: at some point you need to choose a wave and go. If you don't, while you may have a peaceful morning bobbing up and down in the ocean with your thoughts, you didn't do any surfing. It's the same choice you face many times over in the course of your management day.

There's a complex combination of things you have to consider there too: the performance history of each person and the quality of relationship you have with them, the current state in the ever-shifting tide of mood and morale, the dysfunctional leadership and cultural dynamics that are always present to one degree or another, and, most importantly, whether you're carrying extra frustration because you're observing something that you should've addressed long ago. But at some point you have to choose a wave and go. If you don't, while you may see and have all kinds of theories about what's happening with the people on your team, you didn't do any managing.

When it comes to managing a team, the wave is behavior: specifically, the micro-behaviors of the people on your team as they go through their day. Especially relevant are the behaviors that you're constantly trying to make go away: communicating carelessly or unclearly with teammates or with you, poor time and calendar management, hiding weaknesses instead of asking for help, trying to please you and not taking risks, questioning things repeatedly and not getting things done, making projects bigger than they need to be, cherry-picking easy tasks and procrastinating on the harder ones, and on and on. It's ironic that these behaviors, which seem like pebbles in the shoes of your otherwise wonderful day, are the wave, but they are. They are the good stuff, the stuff personal and professional growth dreams are made of.

Most managers make the innocent mistake of starting at the opposite end. They try to address individual performance and cultural issues through group announcements: generic statements about the need to own your work, care more about the customer, be a better communicator, etc. Managers hope that these messages will reach their intended audience, that they will move people to take action and change unproductive behaviors. But they mostly don't. It's not because people don't care or don't want to grow. It's because that's not how growth happens, especially the personal kind. Those group announcements, at best, point to something that needs to change. But they do nothing to show people how to make the changes themselves.

Great management goes in the opposite direction. First, by showing people how specific actions led to specific outcomes, both negative and positive. Then by helping people see how those outcomes are holding them back in their career. And finally, by framing those outcomes in a way where people can see the connections, how the thing that's holding them back at work is holding them back in the rest of their lives in similar, and often identical, ways. The sequence—going from content to context and not the other way around—is everything. You'll see how this all comes together in detail in Chapter Ten, "The Perfect Conversation."

Talking about the behaviors is not enough in and of itself. You can and probably have talked until you're blue in the face about the kinds of things you're about to read. But what you haven't done is connect those behaviors to their impacts, to see them in the context of who this person is and how they're impacting and being impacted by the people and dynamics surrounding them.

In Jon Ronson's fabulous and darkly hilarious book *The Psychopath Test*, which, incidentally should be required reading for every corporate board of directors, there's a passing quote from a psychiatrist who believed he was onto some major discoveries in the treatment of the illness. "There is real hope now that patients are breaking out of their psychological prison of indifference to the feelings of others, a prison that to a greater or lesser extent confines us all."

It turned out that the psychiatrist was overly optimistic, at least with respect to the likelihood of a true psychopath being able to heal. But the rest of the sentence struck me as highly relevant to the challenges of workplace culture. In fact, it might contain the key to diagnosing the health of a company's culture: We could say that *the health of a culture is equal to the collective ability of the people who work there to feel the impacts of their actions on others.* Now if you're an app developer and want to help me build a tool that tracks that, please give a call.

What I've seen over and over again in my career as a business leader and leadership mentor is that this one thing—the inability of people to feel their impact on others—is the cause of cultural dysfunction. And the higher up you are on the org chart, the more problematic that weakness is in terms of what it does to the culture at large. Which is why, as a manager, the most important thing you can do—after recognizing your own impact on your team—is to help people see their impacts on each other, and to help them let go of the emotional story they're telling themselves that's keeping the pattern going.

In my career I've noticed that the kind of impact-producing behaviors I'm talking about here can be broken down into five general buckets, which I'll describe below. They're not hard and fast, often you'll find behaviors that are a blend of a few of the buckets, but understanding them will help you notice them and start addressing them as you go through your day. Because I love a good acronym as much as the next guy, I organized them to spell the word that represents the destination, the feeling you want each person on your team to have, no matter where they are on the org chart: OWNER.

Own the Day

It's 10:00 a.m. The meeting is supposed to start. There are six people on the invite list, but only three are in the room. Those people are making small talk. They sneak a glance at their phones, maybe knock off a few easy tasks. There's no real problem. It's 10:05 and the rest of the group enters one at a time. Pleasantries are exchanged. Phones are checked. One seat still vacant. Where is Mark? Glances are exchanged. Phones are rechecked. People are pinged. Excuses are made. Many things are happening except one: the team getting to work.

Will the company go bankrupt as a result? No. But think like an economist. Think about each of these little transactions, seemingly inconsequential on its own. But multiplied across a team? Across a department? Across a culture? People's relationship with time—and their inability to see how their relationship to it impacts others—is one of the subtle dynamics that pulls teams apart. And it's the first bucket of behaviors where you'll find how seemingly small things have big impacts on everyone involved.

I'm not talking about when something like this happens once, or even every once in awhile. Life is complicated and the last thing you want to do is micromanage people to the point where they're afraid to go to the bathroom in case it makes them two minutes late. You're looking for patterns: someone who consistently puts others in the position of wondering where they are or having to cover for them with others; someone who gives you the repeated signal that they can't be trusted with deadlines; someone who draws you into looking over their shoulder.

Now imagine the alternative, which is what will start to happen when you show people the impact poor time management has and hold them accountable for their part in it.

It's 10:00 a.m. Everyone is ready—they're in their chairs, or standing or bouncing on a ball, for that matter, but they're ready. They've managed their calendar so they're not running here from a meeting they scheduled back to back with this one. They built in time for that five-minute call with their spouse, they took a moment to grab their coffee or tea, they have a clean page open on a notepad (side note: I'm an environmentalist but I much prefer to have people bring a small notepad and a pen than six laptops looking and feeling like a scene out of the old Battleship game).

People are ready to have the meeting when the meeting starts—relaxed, undistracted, and prepared to contribute. There's more space for creative thinking. People get to know each other a little better each day. And you don't have to play the role of anybody's parent.

Walk Your Talk

Have you ever sent someone an email and two days later find yourself wondering if they got it? Checked your sent folder more than a few times to try and figure it out? What's happening, though you may not have considered it this way, is that you're still holding onto the ball even though you think you passed it to someone else. You tried to pass it—to your teammate, a vendor, whoever—but they didn't catch it. They gave it back to you to deal with, *without telling you*, by not responding. What if the situation were reversed? Wouldn't they be anxious for a response to the thing they sent you two days ago, or even yesterday? Communication is one of the most common areas where people don't walk their talk. And it's the way into the second bucket of micro-behaviors where great accountability conversations can begin.

Let's say a member of your team has a Wednesday deadline for a project they're working on. On Monday afternoon, they start to feel that the deadline is at risk. For what may be legitimate reasons—not that they didn't try—they realize they're not going to be able to complete it on time with the quality they know is expected. The professional thing to do is to get in touch with you right then and there. Unfortunately, what most people do in that circumstance is hide. They default to fear and take exactly the wrong path, which leads to frustrated managers and degraded relationships. The key is to not look the other way when they do. It's an opportunity to train, to show them how the choice they made affects you and others, how it makes relationships worse, undermines trust, and takes them further away from the kind of person they want to be. They deserve to hear this firsthand, from you, their boss.

All forms of poor communication have one thing in common: They ask the person on the other end of the line to do more work than they should have to. The accountability pivot is to show them, in granular detail, how that happens *while it's happening* or as soon after as possible. Mentoring your people on how to walk their talk gives them the opportunity to live a life of radical personal integrity, where they strive to embody their values at work in the same way that they do at home, and where they live by this rule: "I'm going to do this right because I want to be the kind of person who lives like that. I don't care if anyone else notices or if I'm the only one here behaving in this way. That is the life I want to lead."

Name the Challenge

Personal growth is uncomfortable. I'm not talking about the kind of personal growth offered up by glossy lifestyle magazines, but the real work of changing ourselves: the vulnerable, embarrassing, uncomfortable, and "Oh god, that thing … again?" Nobody in their right mind likes to see all their flaws in the mirror. What we like, what we want, is the result of personal growth. Which helps to explain why we will do just about anything to avoid the actual process of change—and perhaps will help us all let ourselves off the hook for why it's so hard. The most common way we undermine or slow down our own growth is by covering our mistakes, or minimizing their significance, instead of surfacing them.

We've all internalized powerful, ancient, and often accurate, emotional messages about the need to protect ourselves from authority. Few of us have ever had a relationship with an authority figure whom we haven't had to protect ourselves from in some way. I had a young man on my team once who was going through a horrible situation at home. I didn't hear the full story until much later, but in the middle of a critical multi-month project, the long-standing feud between his mother and father erupted into all-out war.

The people in his world, the people he loved, were doing terrible things to each other. He was an incredibly sensitive and soft-spoken soul, was in a new city and didn't have many friends outside the office, and was being dragged into the middle of his parents' drama. He was wearing it all over himself. Everybody could see it. He didn't want to talk about the content of it at work, which I understood. But what I was able to help him do was just be honest about the context, with me and with his teammates. It wasn't therapy. It was just humanity. "Hey, you guys," he'd taken to saying on days when things were particularly rough, "I'm having one of those days." His teammates did what you would do. They made things a little easier for him in whatever ways they could. They helped him get through it without him having to talk about it or reveal any personal details. The challenge is not solving the problem. The challenge is in being willing to name it.

The belief that sharing our weakness will make others think we're weak is a kind of addiction. And as you've probably experienced, it's an ironic one. Because when we finally stop imagining all the bad things people will do to us, and we actually open up, we learn one of the hardest lessons there is to learn in life: Being real about our limits and weaknesses is the greatest strength there is. It liberates us. The energy and effort we've been using to hide is released, giving us access to new resources we didn't know we had. The acceptance of our imperfections gives us the strength to manage them. And, it breaks down the artificial walls between people, which is why people who work for managers who embody this strength: By being a leader who doesn't have all the answers and needs help from others to grow, are the happiest ones around.

Look around your team. Who is struggling with what? Everyone is struggling with something. Who is running their day assuming their value is based in how many tasks they get done instead of how well they do them? Who's spending so much energy pleasing and flattering because they're afraid someone will see their weakness? Which ones are running themselves ragged every night to avoid going home to a lonely apartment? How can your workplace be someplace where all of these people can belong a little bit more by spending a little bit less time and energy pretending those things aren't true? Look around. Tell them you see. Make it okay. Do it for a thousand days in a row until they believe you.

Embrace Mistakes

If Refound had a break room, the failure to embrace mistakes would be the subject matter of all the cartoons on the walls. "I'm sorry for any inconvenience this may have caused." "We apologize for the delay." And our favorite, "I'm sorry, I promise that won't happen again." Why is it so hard for us supposedly smart businesspeople to say the only thing that will create the result we actually want, which is forgiveness—from our customers, from our colleagues, and from ourselves? Why can't we say: "I really screwed that up. I'm sorry you had to pick up the pieces. I'm not sure what's going on with me that I did that, but I'm going to sleep on it and see if I can figure it out"? It's this simple ownership that we want from others. We can forgive all manner of things when we get it. And it's much harder to move on when we don't.

Most of us have good intentions. In fact, we have great ones. We mean others no harm and want to do our best. But we're not perfect. We make mistakes. We cause other people problems that make their lives harder. And no matter how much we try to avoid it, we hurt other people with our actions or inactions, our words and our silences. But inadvertently hurting other people is not the problem, and apologizing for it is not ultimately the solution—though don't forget to do that too!

The solution is in evolving our relationship to our mistakes. When the people on your team get defensive about a mistake, or try to use the Jedi mind trick on you ("This is not the mistake you are looking for"), start by slowing things down. Find a moment to talk about it outside the heat of the operating day. "Hey I noticed this, don't worry, it's not the end of the world, can we talk about it for a minute?"

Your job is to make it safe for them. Not safe as in no-risk—that planet doesn't exist—but safe as in we're all human here. You can't stop them from feeling embarrassed, ashamed, or a little stupid. What's so bad about feeling like an idiot every once in awhile? It's only a big deal if the person who you're reporting to is pretending they never feel that way.

The potentially life-changing irony is that only by owning up to our mistakes do we learn. Otherwise there's no friction. If we pretend it's okay, brush it off, minimize it to not look bad in the eyes of others, then we miss out on the gap between where we are and where we want to be. Real growth requires that contrast. It can be terribly disempowering to give someone encouragement or cheer them up in a moment when they would otherwise have some space to be disappointed in themselves about repeating a behavior that's obviously holding them back.

If you leave room for people to embrace their mistakes, they'll have room to ask some game-changing questions, like: "Why did I rely on the system instead of using my better judgment?" Or: "Why didn't I act when I knew something was wrong, instead of pretending I didn't see it?" Notice that those questions about work also apply to the rest of life. Figuring out what assumptions are driving your repeated mistakes will make you a better team member, and probably also a better parent, spouse, friend, and so on. If you let people off the hook with an empty apology, you're potentially depriving them of an important learning experience. Stay in there with them. Help them connect the dots. Everybody wins.

Risk Being Right

Most employees assume they have little, if any, power to change the culture where they work. The reality is that few ever try. At least, not in a way that's likely to succeed. Helping them see the impact when they take the risk to be right is another way you can help people understand the role they are playing on the team and the culture as as whole.

It was late on a Sunday night and my business partner and I were poring over the final details of an important choice. We had to decide which coding language we were going to use for an application we were building. On one side was the young upstart—a language called Ruby on Rails—that would give us more design flexibility and greater options for customization over time. On the other side was the current industry standard, which would give us all the things you'd expect: more robust support, more developers who knew the language, and so on. The price difference was negligible. But the new technology was going to be harder and take longer for us to get up to speed and implement.

There was one other thing we knew: The team really wanted to go with the newer technology. They saw its potential, what we could do with it over the long term beyond what we forty-somethings could imagine. It was a tough call but we decided to go with the more conservative option. Our team had other plans.

When we rolled into Monday morning's staff meeting, ready to share the news, we found a piece of paper in front of every chair, some sort of flowchart. What's this, we asked? Chris, a young man on the team, the ringleader if you will, spoke up. "Well, we had a feeling which way you guys were going to come out. And we wanted to give it one more shot. We figured out a way, or at least we think we did, to go with Ruby on Rails, and still adhere to our timeline." We could quickly see that what they'd done penciled out, but told them we needed a few days to think it through. As we walked out of this meeting, which had been a lot shorter than we'd expected, my business partner, who does a great deadpan serious guy, turned around to face them: "You dare to question our Authority?"—letting them know that their victory was very nearly at hand. We had a great company party that Friday night.

We didn't say yes just to reward them for taking the risk. It had to make sense, and it did. But we went out of our way to praise the team, and Chris in particular, for taking that risk. We rolled back the clock in a full company meeting and shared each of the steps that came together to help us arrive at this decision that was going to impact everyone on the team. We wanted to show people what "risk being right" looked like to us.

How can you do that for the people on your team? It doesn't have to be anything as dramatic as the example above. There are smaller opportunities that you'll come across today, and hopefully more tomorrow. Who canceled a meeting that they realized wasn't necessary? Who took the time to give you a simple and clear answer when a more complicated one would've been reasonable to offer? Who gave a refund to a customer, even though it went a little beyond the guidelines, because it was the right thing to do? Who stuck their neck out by coming to talk to you about a friend on another team who was being treated unfairly by their manager? Who put it on the line? No matter how small you think it is, it isn't. It's huge. Show them you noticed. Tell them what it means to you that they did.

You've probably had some ideas pop into your mind already in this chapter, but do a little scan of your team. Which of these buckets does each one person have the most room for growth in? (If you're a coach or consultant, look at how these behaviors manifest in your clients.) Look for the small things. Don't skip the habits that frustrate you or that you know frustrate others on the team. Don't forget about the positive habits either, the little risks people take to go against the powerful conditioning to put their head down and protect themselves. The fuel of all your great mentoring to come is contained in those little moments, the breadcrumb trail that will help you help them to go from where they are to where they can't even imagine they could be.

Learning how to name and work with these five types of micro-behaviors, to use them as ways of starting conversations about larger themes, is the art of great mentoring. It's the gift you can give each person in your world if you're willing to take the risk to try. And, as you can see, it's not about the advice you give or how many times you give it. It comes down to meeting people where they are, at the level of behavior, of action and inaction, in the hundreds of transactions per day that will either help to bring the people your team together or pull them apart.

Before we move on, remember that in one way the stakes are higher for them than they are for you. Even if you both agree that the way they've been doing it isn't giving them what they want, you're still requiring them to examine and change patterns of behavior and long-held beliefs. Being in a position of authority and asking that of another person is uncomfortable, and it should be uncomfortable, because that means you're treating it as the sacred work that it is. The changes we all want don't often come easily. They take trial and plenty of error. It's vulnerable to try, and it may get worse before it gets better. There will be plateaus and they'll last longer than we want them to. But if you stay on it, keep your heart open and your mind sharp, the long-term forecast for everyone is a good one.

Paddle out.

PART II

Personal Growth at Work

CHAPTER SIX

A New Agreement

Change the game, don't let the game change you.
—Macklemore

We are a society in search of healing. And we are searching hard. In Ashland, Oregon, the small college town I live in just over the California border, you can't get to the grocery store for a carton of eggs without bumping into a counselor, coach, or healer of one kind or another. To serve this one little town of 20,000 people you'll find no less than six yoga studios, seventeen acupuncture offices, three organic-heavy supermarkets, nearly 100 licensed therapists (and an equal number of unlicensed ones), along with countless life coaches, nutritionists, naturopaths, chiropractors, and so on. And our town is no exception. This quiet but hostile takeover of the world of healing is in full swing across the U.S., in every city big and small, and on every corner, from Oprah to Omaha.

The business world is now actively embracing many of these ideas and technologies. Fortune 500 companies are offering classes in mindfulness meditation, conscious forms of communication, and mind/body practices like yoga, not to mention making sure to include alternative medicine options on employee insurance plans. And organizations that offer company retreats with a personal growth bent of one kind or another have become a cottage industry unto themselves. There's so much good intention, so many good people trying to make things better. Why aren't they getting better? Is it greed? Is it just the way things are in a capitalist system, with competition forcing people into an un-winnable bargain where they have to treat others in a "get what you can without pushing too far" way? Is the best we can hope for to make things just a little bit better?

Let's return to these questions in a moment and start with a more foundational one: What are we looking for in our quest for healing? It's safe to say that what we're looking for in all of these forms is essentially the same: We're looking for integration. We're looking to recover a sense of ourselves that we feel we lost somewhere, a feeling that our lives are our own, that we belong to a group of people, however small, whose values we share, and that we are making the most of this precious thing called life. We're going to all of these healers and teachers and coaches (who are, of course, looking for the same kind of help from others in their own lives) and, in one way or another, saying "Help. I want to be more of who I am and there's something in the way. Given your training, what do you see about me that I may not? What can I do differently to get closer to where I want to be?"

How many times has an employee ever asked these types of questions of their manager? Isn't it interesting that, despite the frequency and regularity with which our managers see us under pressure, in relationships with others, they are the people in our lives we don't ask—and who, furthermore, don't see it as part of their responsibility to tell us? It's a tragedy of wasted human potential on both sides. How can we get the integration we're seeking if we leave out all the lessons we could be learning about ourselves at the place where we spend more hours of the day than anywhere else?

Into this chasm the voices of company culture have come to try and start a new conversation: the data-driven tool-builders trying to track morale and performance in new ways; the communication-focused trainers and consultants, this author among them, trying to help leaders see what's happening around them with greater clarity so they can take more decisive steps to improve. Everyone who is looking sees the same problem: leaders struggling mightily but still avoiding the risk of being truly vulnerable out of fear of being exploited or taken advantage of; employees on the front lines moving from job to job searching for a feeling of genuine purpose; and managers caught in between, in overwhelm and survival mode, trying to keep a team together long enough to get something done. It's no laughing matter. It's a huge problem, which is why it's also an enormous opportunity.

Before we talk about how to seize that opportunity, we need to get clear on how the trends toward personal healing and culture change are—and are not—coming together. Why, with all this good intention, does it still feel so muddy when we talk about culture, what it is, and how to make it better? *It's because we're trying to bring personal growth and spiritual ideas into the workplace without first changing the underlying agreement that governs it.*

The existing agreement is the one that comes out of the Industrial Revolution, but of course goes back for thousands of years before that: the deeply held belief that work is for the boss. Until we change that, everything else we do will just be a layer on top of the problem instead of a solution to it. We have to try to flip things around, and try and try again until we get it right. We have to figure out a way to change our mindset about what culture change is and who it's for. Ultimately, there can be no cultural evolution until its primary goal is to serve each individual. That's the new agreement. And it's one that employees like David are waiting for.

I met David back in the winter of 2011 at a conference for the previous year's top performers at a mid-size financial advisory firm, the 200 salespeople who'd posted the highest revenues out of their sales staff of 700 worldwide. The CEO, Greg, was a fan of my blog, and hired me to come down and speak on the topic of walking your talk. I'd just finished the keynote and was hanging out near the back of the room answering questions before we broke for lunch. It hadn't been my best talk. I was just starting out on the keynote circuit, still too afraid to let my silly side out on stage in front of a crowd. I was standing in the back of the room when David emerged from the crowd of people milling around and walked over to me with a purpose in his step. He wasn't in a hurry. He was upset. He was a VP at the host company and we'd met over a beer at the hotel bar the night before.

"Hey, Jonathan, can I tell you something?"

"Sure, David, what's up?"

"Your talk really made me angry."

My heart sank. "I know, I know, sorry about that," I prepared to say, but I managed to keep my composure enough to listen instead of talk. "How come?"

"Well, you just stuck your finger into everything that's wrong with our company."

My internal critic relieved of duty, I listened intently as he continued.

"I'm so tired of us hearing all these great ideas that go nowhere. I feel like I'm in a perpetual déjà vu, every quarter a new idea that's going to change the culture. I don't think Greg is doing this on purpose, but it's so obvious to all of us that he's just throwing another thing at the wall and he doesn't really know what to do. Sorry for ranting, but it's so damn frustrating."

"I'm really sorry, David. I wish you were the first person to tell me a story like that."

"Jonathan, I've been with this company for seven years. I guess I just don't know what else to do."

"Why do you think you've stuck around?" From our conversation the night before I knew it wasn't the money.

"*Because I care so much about this place.* I think we could be so much better than we are. If only we would do the things we talk about instead of talking about them."

We continued on for a while, until I asked David a question that took him aback.

"Have you ever thought of sharing some of this with Greg?"

"What do you mean?"

"I mean, you're a VP. You've been here seven years. Why not try and talk to him about some of this? You'll have to find the right moment, and make it clear that you're coming from a place of how much you care and how much you really want to make it about the people who work here. Then let him know you have some ideas about how to make that happen."

"That's what I should do."

We chatted for a few more minutes before David wandered off, seemingly resolved to take the next step. I don't know if he ever did. I'm afraid he did what we all so often do: We assume we can't make change happen, and rather than risk getting hurt, we protect ourselves and swallow our frustration, only to a pay a much bigger personal price later.

David's issue was not with Greg's intentions. He genuinely liked Greg. He respected him and looked up to him in a lot of ways. David's issue was with what Greg saw as his role in the culture change project and his relationship to change it-self. Greg, like every other CEO and leader I've ever met, was doing what he thought was right. He wanted the same thing all leaders want: for people to take personal responsibility for their work; to innovate and take risks to advance the business; and, as he had told me over breakfast that morning, he genuinely wanted to create a culture that supported the personal lives and goals of the team.

What Greg didn't understand was that culture is not content, it's a context. As I'd done in my career, he was trying to change things by adding good culture ideas without first addressing the dysfunctional culture reality that everyone was living with day to day. And that's why he was failing. The team felt the disconnect, no matter what he said or how well-intentioned they knew he was, they were living in a different reality than he was. They were being encouraged to pursue their own goals, but kept bumping up against an invisible wall that only allowed them to stretch as far as Greg's comfort zone. Which takes us to the first of two steps required to change a culture.

Step one: The CEO or owner has to open the door. The only way to do that is to admit that they don't know how. It's a moment of vulnerability. It's only one moment, but I've seen CEOs put it off for decades. All it is is this: "Hey guys, I really want to make this a great place to work. And, as you know, I've tried a lot of things over the years. But the truth is, even though the business has gotten better in some ways, when it comes to the culture—how people feel about coming to work here—I know it hasn't changed in the ways you need it to. *I don't know how to change it but I want to start a new conversation with you about it. Okay?*" Talk about strength. That's the kind of leader I want to work for.

If I were the employee of that fictional CEO, I imagine I'd feel closer to them at that moment, I'd feel some compassion for them, and I'd feel inspired. Not because they had the answer but because they had the guts to admit they didn't. Because, by owning their limitations and allowing others closer, the CEO takes the first step, which only they can take, toward seeing their company as a place to grow beyond what they already know or can figure out. In that moment, the CEO changes the agreement.

Then, and only then, does the CEO earn the right to challenge the team to do the same. It's not that nothing can change without this step by the CEO, but the change project will be hugely restricted without it. Can you see why? Because if the CEO is exempt from the culture-change conversation, that's a clear statement that the organization comes first, that goals and results are more important than the people delivering on those goals, no matter what the company values say or how many inspiring ideas are shared. When the CEO turns the page on the old agreement by changing their personal relationship to it, the culture change project has truly begun.

The second step required to change a culture must be taken by the rest of the team, at every level of the organization. Everyone honors the new agreement that the CEO initiated by taking 100 percent responsibility for their actions. And even if their individual manager doesn't, they honor it themselves by doing excellent work while nobody is watching, caring for the customer beyond what the manual says, and speaking up when they feel a colleague is being treated unfairly, because in doing so they get to feel like themselves.

Personal growth requires risk. It demands vulnerability. It requires that we be willing to be hurt and to accept that we sometimes hurt other people even when our intentions were good. We don't get to look good and grow at the same time.

What we do get is the ultimate gift—a glimpse in the mirror to see how we push others away without realizing it, how we keep our distance and play it safe and then blame other people for doing that to us. And how we sell ourselves out when we put our head down and let politics win the day without taking the risk to say "Something isn't right here. We are better than this."

Personal growth doesn't mean changing ourselves, though that's a part of it. It means letting the people in our lives change us, to help and hold us accountable for pushing aside the ways we've learned to cope, so that we can rediscover the version of ourselves that we know is there but is hard to reach. And the best personal growth is the kind that happens to us in our relationships, especially when the stakes are high, the kind that helps us find the motivation to do the hard thing instead of taking the easy way out. Work isn't the place we should be cordoning off from personal growth. It's the place where we should be diving headlong into it. How we do that, however, is another matter entirely.

CHAPTER SEVEN

THE ART OF CULTURAL LISTENING

> *Listening is being able to be changed by the other person.*
> —**Alan Alda**

We've been talking about impacts, but there's one aspect we haven't talked about fully: how hard it is get out of our own world long enough to be able to see and feel the impact of our behavior on another person, or a group of people. Not how we wished or intended it to impact them, but how it did from their perspective. On the flip side, have you ever had the experience of someone acknowledging fully how their behavior affected you, owning how they hurt you, without in the same breath either justifying what they've done or excusing themselves from real responsibility? It's interesting that no matter how advanced we get in some ways, that kind of genuine apology doesn't seem to get any easier to find. "I hurt you. I can see by your reaction that I did. I'm sorry. But sorry is just a word. I care about our relationship and I want to make it right if I can, so I'm going to figure out what was going on with me that made me think that that was okay."

This is hard to do in our personal lives, and equally hard at work, on either side of the manager/employee dynamic. It's as rare for an employee to make a true apology as it is for a manager. But I've found that there's a unique constellation of things that makes being able to feel your impacts on the culture harder the further up the org chart you are. In this respect, being the CEO is the most difficult of all.

There's one reason for this that strikes me as the most obvious, which is why I'm surprised it's not more a part of the culture conversation. It's this: CEOs are the the only people in the business who don't have a direct experience of what it's like to work for them. They can't fully relate, no matter how hard they try or solicit feedback, to what it feels like to work in the culture they've created. But while CEOs suffer the most from this inevitable blind spot, the limits on our ability to see the culture we're creating on our team is real whether we've got one employee, oversee a department of fifty, or are the CEO of ten thousand.

Marcus was somewhere in the middle of that spectrum. He's the CEO of a well-funded startup that creates apps for wearable technology like the Apple Watch. He launched his firm in 2011. He was 33 at the time, and had just left a director position at a large technology firm. Despite the inevitable ups and downs over the first few years, Marcus and his team had a steadier-than-most rise up to where they are today. People liked what they were building and how they were marketing it, and they were, by and large, a nice company to deal with. In the five years since it started, the company's staff has grown to 65 employees, with only a handful of people who have been there from the beginning.

Marcus is passionate about culture, and he understands its significance. It's no theoretical nice-to-have for him. If you asked, he would say "Culture is everything." He knows that the experience his employees have of coming to work each day translates directly into the experience their customers have, and directly affects his monthly financial statements. He'd written and re-written value statements, a five-year vision for the business, and had a bonus plan tied to short-term and long-term goals. As far as he knew, and from what he'd read online and in leadership books, he was doing everything right.

And he was not alone. At the end of 2014, in what had become an annual practice, the team was given the opportunity to rate the culture. They gave it an 8.9 out of 10. If you walked the halls of the firm, as I did a few months ago, you'd find people smiling, full of life, and excited to welcome a new face into their midst. But something was wrong. Very wrong.

Dale, one of four senior directors at the firm, was away on holiday. In a team meeting that week, Marcus asked a group of managers, at the level below Dale in the organization, what was the thing they felt needed to change most about the culture.

We encourage all our clients to ask this question, even when things are going well. A few different things were shared, nothing that Marcus hadn't heard inklings of before in one way or the other. He made some notes so he could consider their feedback over that weekend and pick up these issues with them in their next meeting.

But something was bothering him. Suzanne, one of his lead salespeople, was uncharacteristically quiet. Though he was hesitant to put anyone on the spot, he took the extra step of asking her if she had something to share. She said she didn't. Still, as he left the meeting, he couldn't let it go. He passed by her in the hall a bit later and asked if she had a minute. They ducked into a nearby conference room and closed the door. The truth came out. I wasn't there, but here's how Marcus reported the conversation to me:

"It felt like there was something you had on your mind but didn't feel comfortable sharing, Am I misreading that?" Marcus asked.

"I'm really nervous to say anything about this, but you know what? You're right, there's no point in sitting on it any longer."

"Any longer?" Marcus's concern started to rise.

"Look, I know Dale is your guy, Marcus … I know you guys go back to college together … but the way he treats us sucks."

"Us?" Now Marcus was really confused.

Realizing that Marcus was really listening and she could finally speak up, she continued: "Women, Marcus. I thought it was just me. I've sat on this for a while, but without naming names, just know that I'm not alone."

"Okay, Suzanne … I'm just trying to take this in right now.

I didn't know … Why didn't you say something sooner? We've known each other for years."

"You don't remember?" Suzanne realized that he didn't. "Remember two years ago when Dale let Jennifer go? Do you remember what you said to me at the time?"

Marcus' heart hit the floor. It all came rushing back. He remembered how he'd blamed Jennifer at the time, how "passive-aggressive" she was, and how the team would be better off without her. They talked for a few more minutes and agreed to reconvene later that day. As soon as he left that room with Suzanne, Marcus did what he does best. He went into action mode. (This is a strength in one way, a weakness in another, but we'll come back to that in a bit.) He initiated some private conversations with other women on the team, told them he was waking up to the issue and that he was going to fix this. He sent me an email expressing his anxiety—and relief—that the issue was out in the open, and his confidence that they could now do something about it.

We spent an entire group video call talking about this one interaction. He was graceful enough to share with the rest of the CEOs in his group, and got some great feedback from the others on the call. But something he said along the way struck me as odd. I'd heard him say it before but the significance of it hadn't registered until that moment. See if you can catch it.

"I'm glad this came out. I mean, we were about to have three senior directors and 25 percent of the staff walk out the door. I'm not kidding. I'm glad we're talking about it all. I think we'll work through it. But something is still bugging me. Why didn't anyone say anything? How is it, after all we've done, that they don't feel safe to bring something like this up with me? I mean I'm out there every day, I don't even have an office, I'm out on the floor right with them. I think our culture is great in some ways, but in another way there must be something really wrong… and I can't for the life of me figure out what it is."

What did you hear? Was there anything that struck you in Marcus's story as odd? Go back and read it again if you like. Try to zoom out in your mind. Imagine Marcus is speaking a foreign language and you're trying to pull out a key word or phrase that will help you understand.

Trying to share my thought process with the rest of group as best as I could, this is what I said after Marcus finished: "So, here's how I'm listening as Marcus was talking. I'm thinking … okay, so there's some underlying dynamic that's causing this. It's not about Dale, though he's of course part of it, but people for some reason aren't feeling safe.…" (I could tell from her facial expression that one of the other CEOs on the call heard what I heard but didn't name it in the moment). As an aside, one of the core things I try and teach leaders to develop the confidence to do is this: If you feel something, say something. You can't lose.

"Can I ask you something, Marcus? There's something that struck me as odd as I was listening to you. Why don't you have an office?"

Marcus put his palm to his forehead in a mix of embarrassment and relief—isn't it funny how often the leadership moment looks just like that?

"Oh my god. They literally don't have a safe place. They can't come talk to me in private because I don't have a door!"

"There's one other thing, actually," said Maggie, the person who'd kept quiet earlier and was now about to one-up my moment of coaching brilliance. (Kidding aside, is there any better feeling in the world than when you're trying to help someone break out of their shell, and they finally take the risk to speak their mind?)

"You're sending another message by not having an office," Maggie went on. "With you being out there every day, I can imagine people thinking, 'Well, Marcus must see how Dale is treating the women on the team and he must be okay with it.'"

Marcus didn't need a last straw, but that was it. As one part, but only part, of the process of moving through this cultural moment, he shared with his team the new insight. The women on the team confirmed that, indeed, they had felt intimidated and hovered over by the senior leadership team, not only Dale but Marcus too. They didn't know how to talk about it because being together seemed so much a part of the company culture.

Over the next 24 hours, the team re-arranged the office. Marcus posted a photo of his new view to his CEO peer group. The culture was on its way to a major healing moment. They experienced firsthand something that's easy to forget in the desire to create collaboration and teamwork: healthy relationships, professional and personal, require a certain amount of distance. Everyone needs their own space. That doesn't mean everyone has to have their own office. There are plenty of creative ways to do it, as Marcus and his team did in a few days using only the spaces and desks they already had. But people need a place to think and to feel at work, and a space to feel frustrated with their boss without having to put a happy face on it.

Creating a private space was only part of it. Marcus had

to prove to the team that the space was also a safe one. He opened up his calendar that week for anyone who wanted to come and talk. Almost everyone did, and not only the women in the office. Marcus had opened the door—in his case by closing it!—demonstrating his commitment to rooting this issue out. He also let his people know that he knew the process was going to take time, and that he would be in it with them the whole way. That said, things started to change fast once Marcus opened up the space as fully and transparently as he did.

Having a place to talk freely did two things. First and foremost, it gave the women on the team a chance to open up about past experiences which up to that point they had felt they had to bear quietly in order to keep their jobs. And in having the opportunity to open up about those experiences, they were able to let them go. Second, that new space did something for Dale. It gave Dale room to do some soul searching, and that's exactly what he did. After a few weeks, he went back to the women on his team, one by one, to apologize. And that's when his own healing happened. He found out that the voices and judgments he'd made in his head were wrong. The women on Dale's team weren't holding a grudge. They weren't hoping he'd get fired or quit. They were quietly cheering him on, knowing the difficult moment he was going through. As one woman on the team, who didn't know the subtitle of this book, said it: They were rooting for him to become the leader they were waiting for.

We are all human. It's very difficult, and usually impossible, to make discoveries on our own like the one Marcus had over those few days. We need others. We need people we trust to point out the things we don't see yet. Asking for help is hard.

Fearing we don't know the right question to even ask keeps us from trying. But that's what it takes to see what is true beyond what we think is true from our individually limited viewpoint. What's actually true is often far simpler than what we imagine, and can have a more profound positive impact on our teams than any team-building workshop or inspiring speech can touch.

Cultural listening is the skill of being able to see beyond the symptom to the underlying dynamic. It's an extremely powerful tool to develop as a leader, whether you're the CEO, a team leader, or a solopreneur just starting out. The more Marcus thought about these issues, the more he realized—as Suzanne had hinted—that the seed for these issues was planted years ago. And even though he was a different guy these days, that kind of cultural history has incredible staying power. What cultural history are you still living with that you can uproot the way Marcus did?

If your team isn't coming forward and challenging you on cultural and interpersonal issues, don't assume there aren't any. Assume that for whatever reason, they've decided that speaking up feels like sticking their neck out too far for comfort.

There are a lot of reasons people might disengage from your team or not speak up. The most common one is feeling like they don't have a voice—that no matter how many times and in how many different ways they try to make changes, their words fall on deaf ears. Keep the Employee Engagement Myths (Chapter Three) in mind. It's not true that nobody cares as much as you do. The conditions are simply not present for them to express their care in a way where they win and you win at the same time.

How are underlying leadership dynamics playing out in your culture? They could be taking a physical form, in the way that the office is structured and where certain people sit, as was the case in Marcus's office. They could be manifesting in the way meetings are held, or who is at them; an arrangement on the org chart where reporting relationships haven't been updated to reflect current reality; something unspoken about communication standards that's causing resentment; and so on. And just remember that even after you address the problem in an outward way, (e.g., by rearranging the desks), your next job is to work on the emotional story that allowed it to be there in the first place so you don't recreate the problem somewhere else.

There are three important leadership skills that we can draw out of Marcus's story, each of which you can develop to improve your cultural listening skills:

1.   Assume the disgruntled employee is a spokesperson.

When Suzanne finally voiced her complaint, Marcus didn't try to shut her down or fall into the trap of thinking she was all alone in her concerns. In some ways Marcus had a strong relationship with her, but it's important to remember that that won't always be the case. Often the richest cultural data will come from a voice that's hard to hear, someone who you get a lot of complaints from or about, or someone you find frustrating for other reasons. They key here is to suspend as much of the background noise as you can so you can hear the message itself.

Without letting them off the hook for their role in whatever the situation is, what's true about their perspective? What are they telling you that you might not hear otherwise? Can you connect their frustration to one of your company values that maybe you're not living up to right now? Out of your own healthy self-interest to make things better for everyone, how can you take full responsibility for the data they're offering you?

Your goal is honest feedback. Your task is to get it however you can, no matter how hard it is to hear. You don't have to be a great leader to know how to do this—by doing this you will become one. How you handle a disgruntled employee will send an important message to the rest of your team about how you relate to dissent. Do you shut it down? Or, so long as the dissent is respectful, can you learn to stand in your center and listen? You might be surprised to find someone you thought was against you is actually deeply aligned with your point of view and can be a passionate ally in your culture change project. Perhaps all they need is an experience that their voice matters. Consider this: Maybe nobody in a position of authority has ever given them that. What if you did?

2. Assume that the problem has collected interest over time.

Discovering a deep-rooted cultural issue can be a huge blessing. As awkward, embarrassing, or uncomfortable as it may be to confront the reality, you have to, because it's already there, de-grading morale, creating the conditions for disengagement, and affecting the overall performance and long-term health of the team. Getting it out in the open and dealing with it transparently can be a transformative moment in your culture, especially for the people who have been trying to bring it to the attention of leadership for a while. It's also a way to reward them for taking the risk to be right at a time when nobody else would listen.

That doesn't mean act rashly. It's easy to jump into action mode too fast when you encounter a cultural problem. Stay in data-collecting mode. Trust that by naming the issue, you've gotten ahead of the game enough and have some time to consider the situation more deeply before taking next steps. A short email, or if you have the venue, a brief announcement in a team meeting is all you need as a first step. "Hey guys, I'm aware of this issue. I'm talking to everyone I can about it and will get to the bottom of it. We'll talk more about it in a few days." This allows your team to exhale, go back to work, and process things in their own way. If you don't try to hide it, there's no story to gather momentum as gossip.

3.   Listen for what they mean behind what they say.

There's another kind of cultural listening that you can work on over time. It's to take seriously things that seem like casual or offhand comments. There's often a gap between what people say and what they really mean. It's not that they're lying to you. It's that they're telling you the truth in a version that they think, or have learned, is culturally acceptable. If you practice slowing them down, you'll find these offhand comments can be magical moments to start a mentoring conversation, to get below the surface of things, which is so hard to do in our fast-paced world.

Here are five of the most common things you'll hear—that are easy to dismiss at face value—that you can use as opportunities to open up a more meaningful conversation.

1. When someone says "I'd like a raise," here's what the emotional story behind that might be: "I don't feel that you really value the work I do here. It's not that I want all the credit, but I want to be acknowledged in a meaningful way for my individual contributions and not just for my role on the team. I've tried talking with you about this but it never really goes anywhere. Asking for a raise is my last resort."

2. When someone says "Can I work from home today?"— or perhaps in your culture it's "I'm going to work from home today"—they may be saying, "This week has been hell and I just need a break. It's so frustrating that we keep bumping our heads against the same wall on this project." That doesn't mean you shouldn't allow that person to have a reset. It means you should also investigate the deeper trend that caused them to be overwhelmed in the first place.

3. When they say "When do you need that by?" what they often want to tell you is: "We have way too many projects going on right now. Can you please clarify where this fits on the priorities list? And it would be great if you could help us clean out the closet on all the half-finished ideas here so they're not taking up so much mental space for all of us."

4. When you consistently hear "Sorry I'm late," you should be hearing: "I just don't feel inspired working here. I'm not sure

what it is, I wanted this job when I first got here, but I go home at night feeling drained and uninspired."

5. When something goes wrong and someone says, "I'm not sure why that happened," consider whether what they're really saying is: "Come on, you know exactly why that happened. It's because _____ did _____ again. When are you guys going to hold him accountable and stop letting him drag the rest of us down?"

What other versions have you heard? It's not about over-reacting to isolated comments. It's that comments are rarely isolated. As a manager, you're getting coded information all the time. It would be wonderful if people said precisely what they meant and why it mattered to them. But that's not realistic given the power dynamics at play when money, career, and our sense of value is on the line. To be a manager is to be part detective. The clues are everywhere, the skill is in reading them.

When you hear one of these coded sayings, or think you might be hearing one, the simplest approach is the best. Ask. "Hey, I notice you've been in late a few times this week. Is there something going on?" Or, "I'd like to have that conversation with you about salary. I'm not making any promises right now but let's put all the factors on the table, including salary, and take it from there."

Sometimes, as they say, a cigar is just a cigar. But usually it's the other thing.

CHAPTER EIGHT

Accountability, A Love Story

*You keep using that word. I do not think
it means what you think it means.*

—Inigo Montoya

I love new ideas. And I love words. And if I have a superpower,
it's the ability to take a new idea and translate it into words that
the first-time listener can relate to. If you like this book so far,
that's probably a big part of why. And it's why I've gravitated
towards the brand and marketing conversation over the years.
But get this: That strength was also what was keeping me from
being great at it. That is, until accountability came to the rescue.

I was in a VP role at the time, leading the marketing team
of a company during a time of expansion. We were looking
to grow our sales qualified leads. As business lingo goes, that
phrase is at least accurate. A sales qualified lead is someone who
you know, based on what you've learned about them up to that

moment, is qualified to buy your product. Said another way: While they may not buy from you, they're in the market for and can afford the kind of thing you're selling.

There are different strategies and tactics for developing sales qualified leads, depending on your marketing philosophy. We were an inbound marketing shop, which meant our approach was to focus on creating high-value and mostly free content, to offer solutions to common problems, and to work on establishing and maintaining our presence as an authority in our market. It's the kinder, gentler form of marketing compared to more traditional approaches, but the core idea is the same. More eyeballs, ideally the right eyeballs, equals more eventual sales.

Inbound marketing is heaven for an ideas guy who loves words. Our job was to publish blog posts, host webinars, make infographics and downloadable tools, and on and on. Anything we could think of to try and help our market—which, in our case, was small business owners—solve a problem they had. As is true in any industry, the possibilities for what you can put out there are almost endless. And it can all be good. It can all be of value. But there's a catch: Even the best content you create won't necessarily attract the customers you're looking for.

A new CEO had come into the business around that time. She didn't come from a marketing background. Her background, the world she knew, was the individual sales conversation—i.e., how to talk with one of those leads in the most effective way once you got them on the phone. The world of inbound marketing—especially given how new the technology and philosophy was in many ways—was understandably outside her comfort zone. That required me to explain things that seemed straightforward to me but weren't to her. And it was driving me crazy.

Each time we'd meet she would pepper me with questions about what was happening at the different stages of the marketing funnel. No matter how many times I explained it, or believed that I had, it didn't help. We'd end up back at the same place, me frustrated and itching to get back to creation mode, and her still feeling in the dark on this critical area of the business. She was justifiably growing impatient, and holding me accountable for the truth. It was my job to put her mind at ease about how our dollars were being spent and what we were getting for them.

I went home one weekend in a stew. Didn't she get how hard I was working? How much we were putting out there? How pretty darn good it was working? By that time in my life I'd learned the value of finding a venue to let that internal dialogue play itself out. I complained to a friend or two until they got bored. I went for a run and found myself running extremely fast. I dreamed of the company I was going to create away from people who "just didn't understand." At some point I started to calm down. And then I had a breakthrough.

It was after dinner on that Sunday night. I was flipping through my notes from a marketing conference I'd been to a few months before. There were so many different pieces, how could I explain it simply? There were visitors—basically, anyone who came to the website. There were contacts, who took the next step and gave us an email address. There were the marketing qualified leads, who'd done the online equivalent of taking a few things off the shelf to have a closer look. And then there were the ones who who kept coming back to look at those products, trying to make a final decision about which one they wanted—those were our sales qualified leads. There's more to it than that, but we were doing everything we could to grow all these numbers. Getting clean data about who was at what stage is harder than it sounds, even with the best automation tools on the market. That Sunday night, not sure what else to do, I thought, "I'll put the numbers on a spreadsheet so they're all in one place and walk her through it again."

And then a wave of inspiration washed over me and I thought: "No. I can do better. A lot better. I can show her the relationship between these numbers. I'm not sure how I'm going to do that in a simple way. But I'm going to give it a shot." In the next few hours I had a steam-bursting-out-of-my-ears work session, parsing data, cutting and pasting numbers, creating ratios between the different elements. In those two hours I hadn't come up with a single new idea about how to increase any of those numbers. But I had come to a deeper understanding of what those numbers meant, and more importantly, how they related to each other. I didn't know if this was what my boss was looking for, but it was for sure different than anything I'd attempted before. I emailed the spreadsheet to her before going to bed, curious what I'd get back.

I stopped by her office Monday morning to see if she'd had a chance to look at it. She had. And she was thrilled.

"This is incredible," she said. "Where did this come from?"

"A moment of inspiration, I guess," I responded in a rare moment of shyness.

"This explains everything. I get now exactly what you've been trying to tell me. Now I can see it in a way I couldn't before. Thank you!"

But that was only part of it. While it was of course a great feeling to have a happy boss, the new spreadsheet and the understanding that went with it helped me and the team far more. It helped us get orders of magnitude clearer on what we were trying to accomplish. We were able to connect each creative project to a specific metric or goal, and track the results of our efforts in a way we'd never been able to do before.

We kept at it, tracking those metrics and especially the relationship between them, over time. I put it at the top of the agenda for our weekly staff meeting. We pulled the numbers apart. We pushed on one to see what the others would do. We tweaked, refined, updated messages, de-cluttered unnecessary steps in our process. We let the numbers teach us what theories to try and which ones to give up on. Our sales qualified leads went up. Dramatically. My team was happy. The sales team was happy. My boss was happy. But that wasn't the most shocking part.

It also improved my love life. I started talking to my wife about the spreadsheet in the evenings while we were getting dinner ready. "We went from 3.2 percent to 3.3 percent in visitors to contacts this week compared to last week." She gave me a look I hadn't seen in awhile. "Get this: Only 4 percent of our leads came from this one page on our site, but, interestingly, 50 percent of the ones who went to that page end up buying." Her smile warmed in a not-PG-rated way. "I love it when you talk about conversion ratios," she said. I was a guy who had spent a lifetime thinking my value was in ideas and words, and now I'd rediscovered myself as a numbers guy. It was in no small way a life-changing moment. And it never would've happened if my CEO hadn't held me accountable—not for making a mistake, but for over-relying on my strengths to the detriment of my team and my goals.

Tracking the data on that spreadsheet—feeling like I was living in it for months—was the hardest thing I'd done as a professional up to that point in my career. It was a daily fight to resist the temptation to go back into idea mode, to let it slip, to take my hands off the wheel so I could go and generate a new idea. And while I'm someone who's always been committed to personal growth, I might never have made that pivot in myself if my CEO had left me to my own devices. Uncomfortable as it was for both of us in the short term, she stayed *on it* with me, and my team did too. They all kept asking questions, challenging our assumptions, and wondering what the numbers were trying to tell us that we didn't know yet. My manager had made it her priority to help me grow. As complex and difficult as our relationship was personally at times, I know she did it out of a desire to help me grow first, and the business second.

Once I'd made the pivot—*once my strength as an idea guy wasn't covering up my weakness on the numbers*—my strength became a strength again. It was no longer a crutch I was leaning on to avoid the uncomfortable stuff. It wasn't a strength with a hidden cost. The numbers and metrics became a framework, a boundary within which my strengths as an idea guy could manifest in a more focused and effective way. That recognition and personal transformation go to the heart of what great accountability looks like. Great accountability is nothing more and nothing less than having the courage to demand that the people who work for you use their strengths in a responsible way.

Learning to see accountability as a tool to help people own their strengths, rather than point out their weaknesses, is the essence of Good Authority. We get there first by changing our worldview, in all the ways you've read up to this point. And what will inspire us to change our worldview is a clear experience of the benefits. Our job as managers is to show our teams the personal benefits of changing, by focusing intently on how they relate to their work, and how that can translate into the rest of their lives. With all the noise and confusion that surrounds us when it comes to company culture and employee/manager engagement, it's this kind of accountability that gives us a way through to the heart of things.

Before we go step by step through how to put this new mode of accountability into practice, we should spend a minute talking about how accountability is most likely happening now in your organization: Chances are it's coming far too late in the employee development cycle, which results in a pattern we've come to call spontaneous management combustion.

Here's what that pattern looks like: You hire someone. You hope that they're going to fill the gap you're seeing on your team. Usually—apart from the rare true mis-hire—they do some things well out of the gate. But while they're doing some things well, you start to see their limitations. Sometimes it takes a few months, but it's usually sooner than that. Some part of it is a skills limit: They don't know everything you hoped that they would. That's a real problem that needs to be dealt with through additional training on and off the job, but it's not the problem that has the biggest impact on the team and on the culture as a whole.

The bigger problem you're seeing is in their relationship to their work. Or, more specifically, how they respond to the challenge of not knowing what they don't know. Here are a few patterns you may have seen that indicate the person you're managing is avoiding their next step of growth: covering up or attempting to brush off the severity of a mistake; hoarding data; embedding themselves as a go-to person (aka: bottleneck) by creating a system or process that only they know how to use; resorting to quick fixes instead of asking questions and looking for root causes; asking for more time or resources beyond what was agreed on in order to complete a project, instead of coming to you to talk about what went wrong so you can work together to improve it; letting tension build with a teammate or between departments instead of coming to you for advice on how to handle it.

When you lack the skills to intervene, to name the dysfunctional behaviors and help people grow beyond them, these problems fester and expand. You start wondering whether someone is a fit before you've taken real action to poke around and find out. You hear the soft complaints from other members of the team but brush them off. You want to be liked, to be seen as nice and caring, and figure you'll give it another day. But it gets worse. And you take it home with you. You complain to your spouse, until they won't listen anymore. You complain to your friends. You talk about it with your fellow managers. All the while, the team is picking up on your frustration. They start wondering what it is you're seeing but not saying. And then at some point, having waited too long, spontaneous management combustion: You boil over in frustration and act out toward the employee. This can happen either directly—through punitive harsh words or action of some kind—or indirectly, by giving them undesirable or less critical assignments, or too quickly dismissing their next suggestion. This usually feels like it's out of left field for the person receiving it.

Not intervening when intervention is called for has a huge impact on the rest of the team and culture at large, because everyone is watching how everyone else is treated. What drags teams down and frustrates your best people into leaving isn't seeing someone being held accountable, it's seeing them not be. And then being shut down, demoted and, eventually, fired without ever being given clear feedback and a chance to grow.

It's equally hard for you as a manager to recover from spontaneous management combustion as, without intending to, you'll likely have undermined the good elements of the relationship that were in place.

The purpose of accountability is to avoid that cycle, to address personal issues and behaviors on the team as much as possible while they are happening. Your goal is to avoid both ends of the accountability spectrum—not too soft and not too hard. Learning the art of great accountability takes time. It's a new kind of conversation that we're not accustomed to having at work. It's not too personal, but it will probably feel that way at first. Just keep in mind, as you've been seeing throughout this book, the goal of accountability isn't to point out someone's weaknesses, it's to help people take full ownership of their strengths.

Great employee development is focused far more on who people are and how they relate to others, and far less on overseeing projects, tasks, and deadlines. It's a conversation that can't wait for quarterly reviews—and oftentimes even weekly reviews are too far past the moment when things are ripe and ready for change. Ideally it starts in a person's first week on the job, and it doesn't end for as long as they're on your team. Your goal is to create a world where mentoring, accountability, and support are the norm. In the next chapter, we'll show you step by step how to achieve that goal.

CHAPTER NINE

MICROMANAGEMENT REIMAGINED

Love sometimes wants to do us a great favor:
hold us upside down and shake all the nonsense out.
—Hafiz

Most of us associate accountability with punishment. We think "Uh oh, I must be in trouble." Our first experiences of being held accountable for our actions, by teachers and parents and the other authority figures of our youth, often came with fear and anxiety. Sometimes they came in the form of raised voices and overt discipline, but often as children we experienced a background anxiety, a worry that we were somehow not doing it right. We carry that story into our adult lives, as employees, managers, and executives on both sides of the accountability equation.

I was on the phone with a business owner a while back who was complaining about the way his team was showing up, making sloppy mistakes and not going the extra mile with customers, having daily communication snafus with each other. On the other hand, he was telling me that he was really strong when it came to holding people accountable. If you ever find yourself in the role of coach or mentor and someone you're trying to help makes a claim about a strength (or a weakness, for that matter), ask yourself if the opposite might be true. We are, myself included, often the worst judges in the world of what we're good at.

"Okay, so let's clarify our terms here. I just want to make sure what you mean and what I mean by accountability are the same thing. So… are there consequences for people when they show up like that?"

There was a long silence.

"Well, um … no, not really. Wait, what do you mean?"

Over the course of the rest of our conversation I helped him see that what he was doing was talking about accountability without implementing or instilling any real accountability in the culture. He shared candidly how he struggled with the exact same issue at home with his three kids, and ruminated out loud how solving this problem at work might help him in far more ways than he originally thought. We can always make connections between our struggles at work and at home, if we're willing to look in the right way. Work is not outside of our life. It's one of the biggest parts of it. Even if the work you're doing isn't the work you want to be doing a year from now, the way you are relating to it is all you, every day. It's now and now and now.

What was happening for this business owner highlights a key element that's easy to forget: As a manager, the more you talk about something without following up with action, the

MICROMANAGEMENT REIMAGINED   99

less those words will matter. The problems get worse instead of better. As the story of Mike and his father illustrated back in Chapter Two, accountability is a profound mirror. Good intentions are not nearly enough. Most managers are well-intentioned people. So were, by and large, our parents, teachers, and the other authority figures of our youth. But that didn't keep us from being terrified of getting in trouble and learning to avoid authority whenever we could, or feeling embarrassed or ashamed when we got caught even if, in the bigger picture, the authority in question was trying to help. We all want to look good, to be seen as creative and hard-working, and it's no fun when someone challenges that picture we have of ourselves, especially if we feel like we've been working on it for a while.

As with all deeply held patterns that we want to change, having a structure to follow as a support can be invaluable. Structure and method are not substitutes for dealing with our emotional world and sorting out a troubled relationship, but they help us frame the problem in a way that makes it easier to solve one step at a time. They keep us from the trap of trying to make big changes overnight, and unnecessarily feeling like a failure when we can't. And since our relationship to accountability was heavily influenced by our earliest experiences of people who were most likely either too tough on us or not tough enough—equally problematic in our quest to become fully formed adults—we need all the help we can get.

The Accountability Dial

The Accountability Dial will help you find the sweet spot in the middle—not too tough and not too soft. As you familiarize yourself with it, don't worry so much about the technical elements at first. Try to get a feel for it on your first read, come back later for the specifics. Focus on the subtler elements—the pacing, the shifts in tone, how boundaries get slowly but surely firmer without ever losing your personal care. By learning to incorporate this method into your management style, you'll maximize the growth opportunities you see for the people on your team by minimizing the likelihood of people getting defensive, either overtly or otherwise.

The Dial is laid out here as a linear process, but don't take that too literally. Customize these conversations based on what makes sense for the current situation. Think of it more as a blueprint for a house. You'll need to make design changes when you get into the individual rooms, as the facts on the ground change, but you have a general idea of what it should look and feel like in the end.

The need to have structure to the accountability conversation is the *why* of the Accountability Dial. The *what* is the sum total of micro-behaviors, people's words and actions that you've noticed over time but have decided not to intervene in for one reason or another. Use the Dial to reverse that pattern—to proactively intervene on things that seem small but aren't, to get out ahead of potential problems. The earlier you intervene, the less likely that people will get defensive. The more real-time and specific your feedback is, the easier it is for people to receive it and learn from it.

The commitment in all the stages of the Accountability Dial is to slow down the moment, since you're going to be addressing behaviors that tend to go by very fast. You'll be mentoring people in a way that's more focused and methodical than most people have ever experienced in a professional context, or even a personal one. At this point you may be thinking, but isn't that micromanaging? Here's the difference; micromanagement is focused on tasks, while accountability is focused on relationships; micromanagement comes from a place of anxiety and fear of mistakes, while accountability comes from a place of curiosity and a desire to help people grow. That's why the accountability conversation will be central to your culture change project.

A final note: As you develop your skills in using the Dial, you will start to surface important themes in the lives of the people on your team—patterns of behavior that are holding them back at work and at home in similar ways. Remember that changing long-held patterns is not easy, even when we know what they are and consciously want to change them. So it's likely that you'll have to go to the next notch or perhaps two on the Dial, to help someone work through a challenge, *even if they're completely in agreement with you about what that challenge is.* For example, you will probably find it valuable and necessary to get to the Conversation (which you'll learn about shortly) to help refine and give more context on something you brought to someone's attention in the Invitation. As a mentor, you have to assume that, just as is true for you, the desire to change—even an expressed commitment to do so— isn't enough. We all need pressure. We need someone from the outside to keep the heat on us, to help us turn the tide in ourselves, by not letting us forget or avoid the issue even though we'd sometimes like to. Because when the going gets tough, the growing gets good.

The Mention

The first notch on the dial is the Mention. It's the skill of noticing a behavior that may not yet be problematic but could become so. At this first notch on the Dial, make your observation with warmth and an open hand. You may have a theory about what's going on but don't assume you're right. The goal of the Mention is to put something into the space for your team member to investigate for themselves. Here's a few examples of what the Mention sounds like in real time:

- "I noticed a few typos in that newsletter that's about to go out. Did you see those?"

- "I saw a flurry of trouble tickets come in overnight. Anything worth talking about?"

- "You seem a bit overwhelmed this week. Something going on?"

What each of these examples has in common is that they're things that could go unnamed. Even if the newsletter went out with a typo, the world wouldn't end (full disclosure: It's taken me many years to fully believe this). Things go wrong with technology and flurries of emails result, and who doesn't feel overwhelmed more than once in a while? The reason you're mentioning what you're seeing isn't to rub salt in a wound or micromanage, it's to give the person you're trying to help a real-time experience of your values and standards. You're using the Mention to show them things like: (1) how keeping an eye on the details is a form of caring for yourself and others; (2) why it's important to try and identify patterns because that's what leads to innovation; and (3) how no matter what's going on in the hustle and bustle, they work for someone who never loses sight of the human beings in their care.

Before we move on, let's spend a minute talking about what the Mention is not. It's not a sit-down conversation, which would make too big a deal of an observation too soon. You're not overreacting by using an intense tone of voice or energizing "I'm the boss" in any way. The Mention is the kind of feedback that could, and often should, happen in the hallway in an off-hand moment, though out of earshot of other members of the team. It's not something to call someone into your office to talk about, though it's a great "Oh, and one more thing …" to add to a meeting that's already on the books that day.

Once you've made the Mention, you've taken the first step. Your next task is to let it go for the moment, and see what the person does with it. If they follow up right away with a question, that's great. Don't assume they weren't listening if they don't respond right away. They may need a moment—in their own time—for what you said to register and spark their curiosity about what else might be going on.

Here are a few things to take a quick snapshot of in the moments after you make a Mention, to complete the transaction for yourself. How intently were they listening? Did they respond first with an excuse or try and pass the buck? Did you notice anything else in their response that made you want to ask more questions? Nothing is conclusive at this point, and you don't need to resolve it here and now. You're simply using your powers of observation and awareness to take a holistic view of what's happening here, and at each step in the process. Now let it go and move on with the rest of your day. By giving yourself this one extra moment you'll ensure that you don't carry any frustration or worry into your next conversation, or even in your body language as you walk back down the hall to your office. Remember, your team is watching you at every moment to decide how safe is it to take the next risk. That's not to make you paranoid. That they're watching is the best news possible, because when you show up with the best of you, they'll notice that too.

Here's what you want to accomplish with the Mention: to plant a seed, but to leave it 100 percent up to them whether they water it, without feeling like they have to do it for you. You're hoping that seed grows, that they'll get curious and come to you proactively with something they learned, or ask a question to get more help to develop whatever skill or ability needs work. Give it day or two. If it's something worth circling back on, it will show up again. By making the Mention, you're making it more likely that both you and they will notice it when it does. When you have at least one more instance to talk about, it's not quite a pattern but it's on the way to becoming one. That's the time to move on to the Invitation.

The Invitation

The Invitation is where you go when you've tried the Mention and the person you're trying to help hasn't picked up the thread on their own. You're turning the heat up here, but just slightly. It's the difference between "Come in, why don't you take a seat?" and "Please sit down." The Invitation should take place in your office, or in some other private space. You're taking the smallest next step you can, picking up on the behavior you named in the Mention and going one step further. You're sketching the lines of a boundary that you can firm up later if you need to. And, most importantly, you're going to ask some questions to try and stoke the fire of their curiosity.

What you're doing differently than in the Mention can be subtle—it's more of a shift in tone than adding a lot of new words or content. The Invitation has a tone that communicates: "That thing I mentioned casually the other day, it looks like you may have forgotten about it, I'm just making sure you know that it's still unresolved from my perspective." During the Mention, you were purposefully not energizing your authority. You hoped that the mere fact of you being their boss would be enough for them to get curious on their own and take a proactive step. With the Invitation you are energizing your authority, just as much as is needed, which is almost always less than you think.

As you move up the dial into the Invitation, you're asking them to look at the same behaviors you asked them to look at in the Mention, but in a way that encourages them to consider the situation more proactively. Here are examples of how you might turn a Mention into an Invitation:

- "Remember that comment I made about typos in the newsletter the other day? I saw a few in the memo to the sales team you cc'd me on just now. I'm concerned that it may be happening more often. Are you moving too fast on things?"

- "You didn't come back to me about those trouble tickets. Did that all get resolved? I noticed the last few days I was wondering about where it went after we talked."

- "Are you still feeling overwhelmed? You seem a little harried still, but maybe that's just me. Has it gotten better? Has it gotten worse?"

One thing you may have picked up on in each example: You're coming from a place of vulnerability. You're expressing your observation in a way that shows you're worried, a little anxious, and that it means something to you that they do something with what you're naming. You might even name that as the context—let them know why you're making what might seem like a big deal out of a small thing. Here's what that might sound like:

"I'm highlighting this because I'd like you to make an effort to listen more carefully to the small pieces of feedback I offer you. I'm not doing it to micromanage you, though I get that it might feel that way. I'm doing it because I want to be able to give you more responsibility and autonomy. And I can only do that if I can let go and trust that things will be handled to the level of care we've talked about. So try to hear these kinds of things in that context. It's my job to ask you questions, to point out little things that you might not see, or might not see as being as important as I do, but it's all in service of helping you grow. I need that kind of feedback too. We all do. Do you know what I mean?"

Before moving on to the third notch on the Dial, let's expand one of the examples to show what a more complete version of the Invitation might sound like. Let's say your Mention went like this:

You: "You seem a little overwhelmed. Anything I can do to help?"

Team Member: "Oh, yeah. I've just got a lot going on I guess. I'm okay, thanks for noticing."

"Sure. Okay, well I trust you're on top of it, and just know I'm here for you if you need me."

Now, let's say you've waited a few days, and they haven't brought the subject up again, but you still sense that things are the same or maybe even a bit worse. They're still operating while being overwhelmed and not asking you for help.

Here's how you might pivot from the Mention to the Invitation:

"Hey, so I wanted to check back in with you. I'd mentioned something about you seeming overwhelmed. You haven't brought it up again, but it seems like it's still a problem. You seem to be rushing around quite a bit the last few days. Am I misreading that?"

"Yeah, you're right. I'm totally underwater right now."

"Why do you think that is? I mean, I believe you that that's how it is right now, but can you be more specific as to what's going on?"

"I just have too many things on my plate, too many projects and not enough time."

"Okay. I know how that feels. So, what are you going to do about that?"

"That's a good question. You know, I think I need to sit down and re-prioritize some things. Everything feels urgent right now."

"That seems like a good place to start. Have you ever tried to do that before?"

"Honestly, yeah—but it helps for about an hour and then I get swamped again."

"Okay, I really appreciate your honesty on that. Can I make a suggestion as to how to approach it a little differently?"

"Sure. I'd love that."

"How about this: Sit down for a few minutes as you planned to do, but instead of trying to figure it all out see if you can frame the question differently, maybe something like this: 'Who do I need help from, or what do I need my teammates to do, or not do, to help me with the overwhelm I'm feeling right now?'"

"Huh, I never thought about it that way before. I can already think of one thing. Anyway, I'll try that."

"Okay, great. I'm curious to see what you come up with."

You've now completed the Invitation. In the example you've just read, it seems like this person is ready do something with the mentoring you've offered. If they do, that's great, and in your next meeting you can debrief what they've discovered and offer whatever advice and make whatever changes are needed from your side. But, as we said at the outset, patterns like this—the behavioral ruts we've all developed over the course of our lives—are not easy to break out of. If you've made the Invitation, and the pattern persists, it's time to move on to the next step: the Conversation.

The Conversation

We're at the critical notch in the Accountability Dial, the one that all of your work up to this point has led up to. It's critical because the Conversation has the potential to go two ways. If it's successful, which is as dependent on your employee as it is on you, it's the place of dramatic personal and professional breakthroughs. If not, it can mean the beginning of the end of their time with your team. Going in, you won't know which of these roads you're on, which is, of course the very reason for the Conversation. This is the moment when you'll bring the best of your Good Authority skills to bear.

Given its pivotal position on the Dial, I've dedicated all of the next chapter, "The Perfect Conversation," to an extended dialogue that embodies what the Conversation can look like. There, I'll highlight some of the key elements to practice and look for as you put the Dial to work for you in the days and months ahead. For the most part, the Conversation is just what it sounds like. You'll schedule a meeting of perhaps 30 minutes, though you may not need the whole time. Make sure your plate is as clear as it can be. Turn off all your distractions. Focus in on this one conversation. This one person. Be the one who cares.

There are two important things you can do to achieve the right balance at this place on the Dial. The first is to stay in a supportive frame. Receiving critical feedback from your boss is stressful. It's especially stressful when that feedback veers into more personal territory, when it's not about a specific skills gap or technical mistake, but about how you're relating to that gap or mistake. Your employee needs to feel that you're genuinely on their side, that the purpose of this conversation is to help them grow, not to punish or shame them. Making use of the Mention and Invitation before you get here is part of how you do that.

The second thing you can do to maintain the right balance is to not try and manage the situation all on your own. The reason most managers avoid the Conversation is that they're afraid of what will happen if this person gets upset and quits. It's the voice in your head that says "Buy they do so much, who am I going to get to handle this if is they walk out?" Just keep in mind that if you're at the point of having the Conversation with someone on your team, this pattern is already having a huge impact on other members of the team (like it was with Cheryl back in Chapter Four). Nobody wins if you don't take the risk to help them see what's going on and move through it. Talk with a peer, check it out with your manager if you have one (or mentor, coach, etc.) and let them know you're about to have a conversation like this and that you're worried how it's going to go. Maybe find a colleague to role-play it with you first. Great managers don't manage alone.

You may want to skip ahead to the next chapter and then come back to review the last two notches on the Dial. Either way, let's reset where we are before moving on. We're moving into terrain that includes the more traditional parts of an employee development process—probation periods, demotions, and termination—but in a very different context: not as a necessary bureaucratic step but as an opportunity for someone to be transformed at a crucial moment in their life.

The Boundary

If the Conversation—which includes follow-up talks and time for the person to work on the issue—doesn't change things, then you have to take more decisive action. You may be more than a little bit frustrated at this point. Projects may be delayed, your peers may be wondering why you're waiting so long, you may be feeling pressure from your boss, but don't give up just yet. There are just a few more steps in the process. Follow them, and whatever the result, you'll sleep well knowing you did everything you could do to help this person grow.

When you're ready to set the Boundary, you should be prepared to let this person go if they don't agree to your terms. You're about to have a sober and serious conversation that requires them to make a meaningful behavioral change in a short period of time. In full transparency, you're going to let them know that if they can't make the turn, they're not going to be able to continue in the job they're in. It doesn't mean they're going to be fired necessarily, it could mean a demotion or some re-organization of responsibilities—which, handled well, can work in some cases. But their job in its current form is on the line. Being in this position is a very difficult part of being a manager, but sometimes a necessary part.

Remember that while the severity of the situation may be very clear to you at this point, it still may not be to them. The Boundary may be a wake-up call, they may *feel* like it's coming out of the blue even if you've done all the right things up to this point. Without losing your focus, keep that possibility in mind. You'll want to customize the Boundary to fit the facts of the current situation, but here's a checklist that can help. Make sure you can answer yes to all of these questions before concluding your Boundary meeting—or meetings, if it takes more than one:

1. Have you reviewed the pattern, and gotten their agreement on what it is?

2. Have you given them at least three examples so they have enough to go on to try and change things?

3. Have you emphasized the impact their behavior is having on the rest of the team?

4. Have you given them your best advice about how to work on the issue—perhaps with a tip or tactic that's worked for you on this issue in the past?

5. Have you kept the door open, letting them know that while this is very serious, there's still room for things to change?

6. Have you scheduled a follow-up meeting to evaluate progress over the next few days?

7. Have you established a clear date by which you expect to see the change start happening?

The Limit

When you've completed the previous steps it's time to set the Limit. Being at this point in the process with someone on your team likely means the end of their time with the company. The Limit is literally your last attempt to help them through this. As such, it requires special care on your part. Getting fired can be a huge blow to someone both financially and psychically, there's often little or nothing you can do about that. But it's also important to keep a longer-term view in mind. Think back on jobs you've left or been let go from. Think about what happened to you from there. Think about similar situations in the lives of your friends, family, and former colleagues. As bad as those times may have been in the short term, and as much as we fear it, being let go from a job—or seeing the writing on the wall and leaving—is often a long-term positive development.

Whatever else is true, they weren't in the right job for where they were in their life. The Limit, and termination if that's where it leads, is part of life at a healthily functioning organization. Take the time to invest your care in the process. It's not only a learning opportunity for them, but for you and your co-managers as well. It may lead you to revisit your recruiting and training processes.

The Limit conversation should be short. It might be only five minutes. You shouldn't leave much space for questions or discussion. Everything that needs to be said should've been said already. If you find yourself feeling defensive or needing to explain, that's a good marker that you may have skipped some of the earlier steps. Assuming you're ready to set the Limit, here's what it might sound like:

"I've been really pulling for you over the last month in making this change. I wish it were otherwise, but I'm just not seeing it. I know you want to change, you've said the right things and I know you've tried. But something is in the way, and I don't know what that is. And I can't wait any longer. What I'd like you to do is to take the weekend and really do some soul searching. I would invite you to ask yourself questions like 'Is this really the right job for me?' 'Is there something else I'd rather do or someplace else I'd rather be?' 'If I wasn't afraid of losing the paycheck, what would I do?' I know these questions may sound strange coming from your manager, but if you can ask them and be honest with yourself about the answers that come, one of two things will happen, in my experience: You'll either come to a major breakthrough about the things we've been talking about, and I'm open to hearing about it if you do. Or, for whatever reason, you'll realize it's just time for us to shake hands and move on. Will you give it the weekend to think about all this, so we can finish this conversation on Monday?"

Based on what they come back with, you'll have all the information you need about what to do next: give them another chance, or complete the process and move forward with termination. Trust your intuition and be willing to be wrong at the same time. That's the high art of management.

Now that you know the five steps for holding people accountable, why not share them with your people? There's no reason to keep the process a secret. Once you describe the Dial to employees who are having a difficult time, you might be surprised to find out that they can immediately locate themselves on it. This kind of transparency might be just the thing they need to realize how big a deal the small moments of the day actually are!

Is It Worth It?

I can imagine many people asking themselves, is it really worth it? On the surface, the Dial looks like a lot of work. Depending on your previous history, it may also look like giving people too many chances and wasting time in the process. I'd like to conclude with a short anecdote to help convince you that it's worth the investment.

I'd decided to let James go. He was a junior sales associate in a software company I was working for. This was years ago, before we invented the Dial and had the steps written out like you've just read. But, without any formal training, this was the process that I had more or less made up along the way. Over the course of a month I went through the process with James, and, in the end, made my decision to let him go. A few days later, at a restaurant near my house, I bumped into one of our developers, a friend of James' who worked in a neighboring department.

"Hey, Jonathan."

"Hey, Amber, nice to see you."

"So, I just wanted to say I know letting James go was tough. But I think you made the right decision. I think it's cool how much you guys tried to help him, I've seen other managers do similar things over the years here and I think that says a lot about our culture. It's sad, but, it's … I don't know. It's also just real."

"Thanks, Amber, I'm glad you could see it that way. It's the worst part of my job. I wish I never had to let anyone go. But it's nice to know you feel that way. I'll sleep a little better tonight."

Every employee you've ever hired wants to do their best. They want to get promoted, make more money, feel more creative, and have a bigger impact in the world. And it doesn't always work that way. Sometimes the best thing you can do for someone, and your team, is to let them go. But before you do, why not try everything you can? What's a few more weeks in the grand scheme of things? If, in the end, all it does is show the rest of the team how much you're willing to help someone grow, isn't that a win worth fighting for?

CHAPTER TEN

THE PERFECT CONVERSATION

Love's in need of love today,
Don't delay
Send yours in right away
—Stevie Wonder

As we promised in Chapter Nine, here's an example of the third notch on the Accountability Dial, the Conversation. This dialogue is a combination of a role-playing exercise I did with a CEO, Catherine, and the actual conversation that followed between her and her VP of Sales, Meredith. As with all the other stories in this book, the names and details have been changed, but this dialogue comes out of a real-life situation and shows us a set of universal themes. On the surface, this is about the lack of accountability that Catherine sees on Meredith's team. She's tracked it over a few months. She knows it's a pattern and not a one-off thing. She's seen Meredith take on other people's work, get lost in fixing their mistakes, and burn herself out in the process. She's brought it to her attention in small ways using the Mention and the Invitation, but the pattern is still there and it's reached a critical mass that's showing up in a variety of ways—morale, customer complaints, and so on.

There's a lot going on in this conversation. We've been highlighting different elements of it in earlier chapters, and we'll continue to in chapters still to come. For now, try to soak it in. Imagine yourself in the room. You may want to read it one time through imagining you're Meredith, and then go back through as if you're Catherine. At the end of the dialogue you'll find "What Just Happened?," where we analyze some of the key moments.

Here's the Conversation:

"Hey Meredith, I know we've been talking about it in different ways, but I'm still seeing your team having issues with accountability. Do you notice that?"

"Um. Well, kind of ... yeah, it's frustrating to me."

"Okay, I believe you ... it's frustrating to me too ... have you given any more thought to why things aren't changing?"

"Well I think we need some better procedures, some more clarity on standards, I think that will really help."

"Okay, I'm sure that's true to some degree, we could always make those things better ... but is there anything else you think that might be causing it?"

"I'm not sure. I feel like I spend a lot of time talking with the team about owning their work, watching out for careless mistakes, caring about the customer, etc. Maybe I'm doing something wrong."

"Could be, but let's not think about it in terms of wrong or right. We're just trying to get to the bottom of it so we can change things, okay?"

"Okay, yeah ... I guess I'm just nervous because I know how bad it's gotten lately."

"Ah, that's such a relief, Meredith. Can you imagine what it's like in my shoes seeing things getting dropped and then wondering whether you're noticing what I'm noticing?"

"Wow, yeah ... I never thought about it that way. Sorry about that. I'm going to come to you sooner from now on."

"Okay, I appreciate that. But let's see if we can go deeper here, okay? I have a feeling that I can help you with something in this dynamic too? I'm not sure what it is yet, we have to dig together, but I know from my own experience that when an issue comes up with the people who report to me, there's a learning experience for me somewhere in there too. Are you up for that?"

"Sure. I mean, I'm not sure where this will go, but sure."

"Okay. So, let's start with what we know. First, we know—or at least, you and I agree—that there's an issue with accountability on the team. Second, we know that while they could be improved upon, we have systems and procedures in place that someone doing good work would be able to follow. We good so far?"

"Yep."

"Okay. So if we assume for a moment that there's something else going on ... there's some background dynamic at work ... what might that be?"

"Well, honestly ... I think I'm not very good at holding people accountable."

"Okay! Now we're talking. Thanks so much for opening up to me about that. I'm sure it wasn't easy. Holding people accountable is not fun. So, tell me more about that. What does 'not good at it' look like?"

"Well, I think what happens is that I end up doing too many things for them. As long as they get it partway done I call it 'good enough' and I bring it home for them."

"That's great self-awareness. Okay, so imagine you were in their shoes. I know it's hard because that's not your thing—you're precise and on it—but if you were in their shoes, what would that be like?"

"Yikes. Well I guess I would start to get lazy. I would feel like I don't really have to do a great job because Meredith will pick up the slack for me."

"Okay, I agree ... I think we're really getting down to it now. How is this so far? I know it's not a fun conversation but can we go further?"

"Oh my, yes. Honestly, this is something I've struggled with my whole life. The more we talk, the more I realize I've been doing this with my husband, with my friends, holy cow I think this is everywhere."

"That's a huge moment, Meredith. And, in my experience, that's the key. When we can start to make the connections, to see the impact of our behavior—innocent as it may be—on others, we're on the path of real change. And you know what else?"

"What?"

"Me too."

"What do you mean?"

"I've struggled with this exact same thing my whole life. *I still do.* I want to be liked, I worry about the things people say when I'm not around. More times than I can count, I've chosen the comfort of fixing the problem over the challenge of helping someone grow. But, I've been working on it a lot in the last few months. And I'm starting to see things change. Which is the only reason I think it's fair that I'm having this conversation with you, *because I'm not asking you to do anything that I'm not asking of myself.* And that wouldn't have been true three months ago."

"I'm touched. I mean, I've never had a manager talk to me like this. Thanks for sharing that with me. It makes this whole thing a lot more real and feels possible in some way that it didn't before."

"I'm so glad. Okay, now let's keep going."

"Alright."

"So, let me ask you another question. Let's assume you're right, that when you take on too much the team takes on a little bit less than they should, and that this pattern has built up over time. Here's my next question: What is that like for you?"

Long pause. "It's really hard, honestly. I feel like I'm at a loss as to what to do, how to get them to change things. I feel like I spend my day chasing the tail of this thing and never catch it."

"Okay, but my question is a little bit different. Forget about the team for a moment. Forget about the business. I know that sounds odd coming from me, but trust me ... we're almost there. How is it for you personally to be in this position with them, having to chase them to do work that's up to your standards?"

"It's horrible. I cry myself to sleep half the week and lie awake the other half. I wanted to talk to you about this but, well, I really can't afford to lose my job."

"Meredith, nobody is losing their job … least of all you. I get the fear, but I'm here to tell you that's not what's happening. The reason we're having this conversation is so you can go home feeling good about things. And of course, I'm interested in sleeping better at night too! … and I suspect that our team has room to grow that you can open up for them."

"Me? How can I do that?"

"Okay, so let's go back to the beginning. If today you're taking on too much and, as a result, they're taking on too little, what might happen if you reverse it? What if you started to take on less, with my guidance on how to do that in an effective way. What do you think the result would be?"

"Honestly, I think some people wouldn't make it. If I scan the team, I think about half of them would take up the challenge and start changing things, but the other half we'd have to have some tough conversations with and we might lose a few of them."

"I couldn't agree more, Meredith, with one caveat. I think neither of us actually knows who is going to be in which half. Because—and this is as much on me as it is on you—we haven't yet as an organization challenged them enough to find out."

"I wouldn't know how to do that."

"Great! That's exactly it, Meredith. That's the gift. Can you see how if you work on something that matters to you, that will make your life better, and it will make their lives better in the process?"

"Yeah, but that feels selfish. I mean, if I don't know how to do it then shouldn't you find someone else who can?"

"What if I told you that I don't know how to do it either?"

"Huh?"

"Seriously. What if I told you that I don't know how to do it either, I don't know how it's going to work out, but I want to do it anyway."

"I'd say you're very brave."

"Fair enough, you could see it that way. But what's more true for me, Meredith, is that I'm in pain. I don't like worrying about everyone here so much. I don't like worrying about what's happening with our customers. And, having known you for the last five years and having seen the personal toll it's taken on you, I want to help you with this problem. That is more important to me than whether we hit our monthly profit goal. Can you let that in?"

"I don't know what to say. I'm just feeling really grateful for this conversation. I know I have a lot to fix, but I just feel like I can breathe a little bit having all of this out on the table."

"I know exactly what you mean. That's what I'm learning about myself lately. That it's not the problems and the frustrations that are actually driving me nuts. It's my trying to bottle them up instead of naming them, talking about them, and trusting that there will be a way through if I take the risk. Recognizing this is having a profound effect on me personally. Not that I'm an expert, I'm just starting to get the hang of this. But I want this for you too. We can do great things here."

"This is inspiring. I think the team would love to hear you talk about this stuff more with them."

"Yeah … I think you're right. Thanks for saying that. I do need to talk more with them about this stuff, they need to hear it from me too. Let me think about how to start doing that better, but if you see some opportunities will you let me know?"

"Definitely, I will."

"Okay, so let's start winding this down for today. We'll come back to it next week, or sooner if you want, just let me know. But let's summarize what's happening. Can you do that?"

"I'll give it a try. So, the reason the team isn't owning their work, at least one of them anyway, is that I'm kind of enabling them. I'm letting them off the hook. And if I learn to hold them accountable, that will create more room for them to execute what they're supposed to. It will put pressure on them, a good kind of pressure, to take ownership of it for themselves. And we'll have to work with each person and mentor them the way you're doing with me. That it?"

"Perfect. That's great. I just want to add one piece to it for you to take with you. The way I see it, what we're talking about is not business or personal. It's both. It's a pattern that you've learned in your life—we each have our own version of that—for how to relate with your work and with other people. All I'm pointing out is how that personal challenge is showing up in a way that impacts the business. These are the ground rules of this conversation from my perspective. Ultimately, it's none of my business how you go about working on this issue in yourself—though I'll help in any way I can—but it is my business that you work on it. And it's my job to hold you accountable for changing it over time. Not all in a day, but slowly and surely. Can we shake hands on that?"

"Yes, and I'll just say I'd love your help with this. This could change a lot of things for me."

"Okay, I'm in. So, here's my proposal. For the next six weeks, that's what I want your weekly meeting with me to be about.

I'd like you to start coming up with a plan, could be some big things but better to be small things. The little steps you can take to start giving responsibility back to them. Okay?"

"Okay, I'll do that. That sounds cool, and it would be a huge relief if I could figure out how to do this. I always hear that phrase 'lead by example' and maybe now I'll have a chance to do that."

"That's it. And how is this, specifically, you leading by example?"

"Because I'm learning to hold myself accountable for changing! And if they see me doing that then maybe it will rub off on them."

"Exactly. And what I'll say is that it won't just rub off on them … it will inspire them. Do you know why?"

"Inspire them? No … I don't get it."

"Meredith, do you think your team knows this about you, that you're somebody who takes on too much to their own personal detriment?"

"I never thought about it but yes … I think they do. Sometimes they say things like 'You should take a holiday,' that kind of thing."

"Okay, so just flip the tables and imagine for a moment something you know about me that I struggle with. Let's assume for a moment that you've known it about me for a while, the stubborn pattern in me, and then all of a sudden you see me changing it. How would that make you feel?"

"I'd think, well if she can do that …. well I can do it too."

"That's how it all comes around in my view, Meredith. It's my job to do that for everyone here and it's your job to do it for everyone here too, but especially the people who report to us directly."

"This just became a much more interesting place to work."

"Isn't that cool? That the things we all need to work on, personally, are so directly tied to the outer results we're struggling to reach? As you can see, I'm focused on these dynamics in a new way. We'll just take it step by step and we'll get there together. We can do this, okay?"

"Okay."

"And Meredith?"

"Yeah?"

"Thanks."

What Just Happened?

Let's highlight some of the key moments in the conversation and zoom in a bit so we can see how Catherine was applying some of the principles of Good Authority along the way.

1. Notice how Catherine starts off in an open way, and asks Meredith if she's noticing the same behaviors rather than assuming that she is.

2. Catherine doesn't reject Meredith's proposed solution about better systems etc., but maintains her focus on the context/cultural issue. Meredith's response that the problem can be solved with better systems is a common

potential pitfall. Though they may know there's more to it, many leaders stop here and follow the solution that's being offered up, instead of pushing further into what can be uncomfortable territory.

3. She takes the time to unpack stock language: "What does 'not good at it' look like?"

4. She takes the time to reframe so Meredith sees the conversation as progress rather than punishment or an opening for Meredith to feel bad about herself: "...let's not think about it in terms of wrong or right. We're just trying to get to the bottom of it so we can change things, okay?"

5. By being transparent about her relief to know that Meredith gets the gravity of the problem, Catherine shows how much it means to her that Meredith is taking the issue seriously.

6. Catherine keeps pivoting from content to context, from easy or quick solutions in favor of deeper and potentially more systemic ones—a key element of walking her talk.

7. She has a theory based in her previous relationship with Meredith, but does her best to lead Meredith to it rather than push it in her face: "I'm not sure what it is yet, we have to dig together..."

8. She was fortunate in that Meredith came to the table knowing something about the issue, and didn't get defensive. (Using the Mention and Invitation helped.) But if she had gotten defensive, Catherine would've needed to back up and spend more time setting this conversation up before going further.

9. Catherine checks in with Meredith —"How is this so far?"— to make sure the conversation isn't going too far too fast.

10. The moment of success is when Meredith has her "Ah ha!" and makes the connection between her pattern at work and her pattern in the rest of her life: "The more we talk, the more I realize I've been doing this with my husband, with my friends…"

11. A key moment: by showing vulnerability with Meredith in owning her own issue, Catherine gives Meredith a model of how to have the same kinds of conversations with her team: "That's what I'm learning about myself lately. That it's not the problems and the frustrations that are actually driving me nuts. It's my trying to bottle them up and 'manage them' inside of myself instead of naming them, talking about them, and finding ways through them. Recognizing this is having a profound effect on me personally."

12. When Catherine says " … How is it for you personally to be in this position with them, always having
to chase them to do work up to your standards?" she's
inviting her to notice how what she's doing is making
her feel bad in and out of work, and that a solution for
the business is also going to be a personal one.

13. Notice how the frame, even when there are personal themes being addressed, stays professional. It's
about the work. Catherine and Meredith are talking
personally, they can talk about feelings and tears
(or anger, etc.), but it is not personal in the sense of
going into the content of her private life or family
history. And Catherine doesn't try to process those
feelings with her, which would be out of bounds in a
professional meeting.

14. Notice Catherine's response toward the end when Meredith owns how she's not sure and doesn't know how
she's going to do it. "Great!" she says, reinforcing that
in her culture she's looking for Yoda-like managers and
not expecting Superheroes who have all the answers
and do it all themselves.

What made this Conversation so successful was Catherine's
willingness and vigilance to stay in the context. She let the easy
answers come and go without shame or judgment. She saw that

her role was not to be the one who has the right answers, but the one who asks the right questions. She held the space and didn't fill it with her opinions and instructions. In other words, Catherine found the strength to not try and change Meredith but to engage with her: to bring all of herself to the moment. She gave Meredith everything she needed to make the change for herself. Wouldn't you love it if someone had a conversation like this with you?

PART III

More Yoda, Less Superman

CHAPTER ELEVEN

More Yoda, Less Superman

*Tell me, what is it you plan to do
with your one wild and precious life?*
—Mary Oliver

Remember that scene in *Superman* where he sat down after the valiant rescue to make sure the person learned from their mistake so he didn't have to come back and save them again the next time? "So, Lois, let's review what happened last night. You wandered over to the abandoned factory, again, right past the sign that said 'KEEP OUT! Evil Genius at Work,' and decided to go in by yourself. Can you walk me through your thought process on that decision? My fear is that you've gotten so used to relying on me to swoop in at the last minute that you're not thinking clearly. Do you know what I mean?"

Of course, there was no scene like that in *Superman*, or *Iron Man* or *Thor* or any other superhero story for that matter.

Because a scene like that would burst the myth of the super-hero itself, a version of the very same myth that I'd shared with my mother's Psychology 101 class all those years ago, the false belief that what makes us valuable and gives us our authority is our ability to solve problems and reach goals. But if you want to change your culture and create conditions where people take ownership for themselves, that's exactly what you need to do. You need to confront the version of that superhero myth that lives in you. What I've seen over the years is that this inner superhero takes three common forms, which we'll explore in-depth in the next chapter, "Fixer, Fighter, or Friend?" Before we go there, I'd like to share with you a moment from my own career where I began to see the outlines of one of those styles in myself: the Fighter.

This was a few years back, when I was leading the marketing department of a consulting business. We had several products that we were responsible for marketing, but there was one in particular that we were focused on at the time. It was a coach training program, one we'd been offering for a few years, so it was still fairly new to the market. We were looking to broaden our reach to a new audience, people who didn't already know about us from being on our mailing list over the years. We were covering all the marketing basics already: a blog on best practices that coaches looking for new skills could use as a re-source, free educational webinars, downloadable worksheets, and so on.

But we felt like the program had the potential to reach more people, and that we hadn't quite communicated what it was about in the clearest and most compelling way we could. I felt like there was something that we could do to take it to the next level, but I wasn't sure what that was. In a moment of inspiration, I decided to bring the team together for a day-long creative session. The plan was straightforward. We'd find a day where everyone could clear their calendar, lock the metaphorical doors, and do some blue-sky thinking. My team was an incredible bunch, a great balance of creativity and pragmatism. I was confident that if we put our heads together something great would emerge.

Emails were sent, calendars were adjusted, and the date was set. The team, myself included, was looking forward to having the creative space blocked out away from the normal little-bit-of-this, little-bit-of-that task-switching routine that is so hard to break out of in a modern business environment. The week went by, and there I was, lying in bed the night before the big day, ready to fall asleep. But my mind was not cooperating.

I tossed and turned for a while. What was I so worried about? Was I afraid we'd come out of the day empty-handed and it would be a waste? Did we do enough planning going in? And then it hit me. The problem had nothing to do with the meeting itself—we had a fine-enough plan and the right people in the room—except for one. "You're not supposed to be there," said the voice in my head.

"Huh?" I replied, a little slow on the uptake. But the voice was very good at sales.

"You're the one always talking about how great the people

on your team are; how creative, smart, and earnest they are. Are you saying they can't do this without you—that without your ideas in the room nothing good will happen? Doesn't that strike you as a little bit arrogant?" Ouch.

At 1:00 a.m., after a few more failed rounds at trying to win the battle to fall back asleep, I figured a little bit of action might put my mind at ease. I sent a note to the two senior managers on the team: "Hey guys. Bit of a change of plans. I know this is out of the blue, but I'm not going to come to the meeting tomorrow. I want to tell everyone why, so nobody has to wonder, so I'll come for the first 15 minutes and do that, but I'd like you guys to lead the day, okay?" I met with the two of them first thing the next morning to go over some logistics and make sure they were on board. I saw a short flash of anxiety come across both of their faces—"What if we can't do it without him?" —but it was quickly replaced by a palpable excitement about the opportunity ahead.

My phone rang at 1:00 that afternoon. They'd broken for lunch and were down the block grabbing a bite to eat. "Hi Jonathan, do you have a few minutes to come by and see what we've come up with so far?" I could tell by the sound of the voices in the background that it was going to be good. They walked me through a few wireframes (skeleton sketches of what a new website they envisioned could look like), the notes they'd been furiously working up and revising along the way, and their estimate of how long they thought the project would take to complete. Up to that moment, my expectation was that it was going to take two months to design, build, and test the new site. But they had increased the scope dramatically. It wasn't so much that they wanted to do more, but they wanted to spend far more time on the little stuff, the user experience of clicking through the site, the micro-copy, all the things that turn an average website experience into a delightful one.

"How long will it take before it's live?" I asked, holding my breath. "We can do it in six weeks," they said confidently. They were wrong. They did it in just over four—in large part because their inspiration spread like a virus. They enlisted peers from other departments who they needed help from. They showed them how this project was for their benefit as well, addressing some of our developers' concerns around the overall stability and flexibility of our online platform.

It's not that I wasn't part of the process. It's that I did the one thing that I'd struggled to do up to that point in my career. When it came to the creative part of it—the ideas, the positioning, and the visual concept—I got out of the way. I trusted them to come up with ideas that were better than the ones I could come up with on my own. I started embodying the thing I'd uttered words about over and over—I stopped acting as if they didn't care as much as I do. Over that next month, I used that freed-up mental space to mentor them on the many challenges that came up along the way. But here's the key: Those were their challenges now, their obstacles to overcome. This was their victory to achieve. They owned it. I still had my say in the direction and could've intervened at any point if I felt like they were going down the wrong track. They weren't. And the result far exceeded the original goals we had for the project. And, while the press was not without a few late nights and last-minute glitches, we had a lot of fun getting there.

The day after that first meeting, the one I had bowed out of, one of the other members of the team stopped by with a knock on my half-open door.

"I just want to thank you for that meeting yesterday."

"Oh, you're welcome, I guess … I didn't do anything … what you guys came up with was outstanding."

"Oh, no … you're wrong," he said. "Your presence was never more felt than in your absence. We felt you with us, supporting us, the entire time."

Ah, that pesky voice in our heads. The one who thinks the only way we can contribute is by having the answers and willing ourselves to the goal.

Let's spend a minute going back to what I did do during that time. As you can imagine, there wasn't a straight line from the meeting that day to a stunning new website. There were a hundred turns in the road over that next month where decisions had to be made, compromises negotiated, more or fewer resources allocated in a given area than originally planned. And while there wasn't any shouting, there were some heated arguments and plenty of smaller tensions and conflicts that came up. The team was working fast. Team members had different working styles, unique personalities, and were at different stages of their careers. My job, the job that I decided to take on during that time, was to be a resource for that part of the project, for the personal side of it.

It's this side, what I'd call the Yoda side of leading a team and helping the people on it, that I was learning how to do for myself.

If you think back to the original *Star Wars* films and those lovely scenes in the swamp—the conversations, the training, and the overall vibe—you already know what it feels like. What Yoda did was open and hold the space for Luke to learn. He shared his wisdom, but only inasmuch as Luke was willing to listen. He gave him challenges that he knew he'd fail at on the outside, because of the place he knew Luke had to find on the inside. And, in the end, he let Luke decide whether he was ready to take on Darth Vader. Yoda wasn't sure Luke was ready. In fact, he was pretty sure he wasn't. But, in his best Good Authority moment, he chose to trust in the outcome and respect Luke's choice.

In a larger sense, what Yoda has to teach us about managing and leading people has more to do with what he didn't do than what he did. He didn't give Luke the answers. He had the emotional strength to let Luke struggle through and not jump in and save him. He didn't try to be Luke's friend and tell him everything was going to be okay, or give him a gold star for trying. He didn't save Luke from the pain of failing until he got it right. He didn't scream or yell or call Luke an idiot. In short, he stayed by his side, invested the best of himself in this one young man, and waited to see what would happen. He had a theory about Luke's potential. But he had the wisdom to know that his work would be wasted unless Luke discovered that potential for himself.

How can you put these ideas into practice with the people on your team? I wasn't thinking of it in these terms at the time, but when I look back, there were four specific tactical things I was doing and that you also can do as you move forward from here:

1. I made sure I had enough openings on my calendar, and wasn't jammed with back-to-back meetings, so that when people came by my office I had the time and head space to listen.

2. I insisted they each keep their weekly individual meetings with me, even if—especially if—they were feeling overwhelmed that week, because I've learned over the years that when we say we're overwhelmed, what's almost always behind that is something we don't know how to do that we're afraid to ask for help on.

3. I stayed in proactive communication with my peers running other departments to make sure nothing went off the rails between us or our people, not so much to protect my people but to protect the creative space that we'd worked so hard to open up for them.

4. Most importantly, I asked questions instead of giving answers. Here are some of them:

   "I'm not sure. What do you think?"
   "What would you do if I wasn't here to ask?"
   "What are you afraid will go wrong if you take that risk?"
   "How does what you're struggling with right now relate to the long-term growth theme we've been talking about?"
   "What are you doing to take care of yourself and not get burned out?"

And, as always, it's not the questions themselves that make the difference. I've seen many managers try to use strategies and tactics along these lines—saying the right words without coming from a genuinely caring place—and have it backfire. There's no substitute for doing the leadership work on yourself so that these kinds of questions emerge naturally in the course of the day and don't come across like canned management speak, albeit a more enlightened version than the historical kind. The words do matter, but who they know you to be is far more important.

Superman's Dread

Here's the last and most important part of my story. If I've made this moment sound easy, let me clarify things. It wasn't. Pulling back my inner superhero—my strengths as an idea guy, my ability to drive and push things forward, my ability to negotiate for resources, all the things I had come to rely on over a twenty-year career leading up to that day—was hell. The morning I waited to see what they'd come up with without me was full of nervous thumb twiddling, email checking, and pretending to be calm. Not because I was afraid that they wouldn't do a great job, but because I was afraid that they would. And then what?

If they could do that without me, then what was my value? What am I being paid this big salary for if it isn't for those strengths? Didn't I just make myself completely replaceable and disposable? I can't wait for you to have this moment. Not because I'm a sadist. But because you'll have reached the first major milestone on the road to becoming a Good

Authority—you'll have fallen into the existential pit of leadership despair. Don't worry, it's not as bad as it sounds.

The first big upside is this: While Superman got a lot of press, Yoda had a lot more time off. Superman worked crazy hours, all that racing around looking for a phone booth. True, he did a lot of saving, but he also did a lot of disempowering. He didn't know, like I didn't know, how to leave enough oxygen in the room for other people to grow. Now I can look back and laugh, seeing all the moments in my career where, by trying to be the hero, I created the opposite of the result that I wanted—or at least not as good a result as it could have been. It's the very act of saving people, or trying to, that disempowers. It shuts them down. It invites them to play it safe and wait. It causes them to say to themselves, "I don't have to step up because he/she is going to swoop in and save the day anyway."

Putting Down the Cape

Making the pivot from Superman to Yoda starts with an acceptance: The strength that got you this far has become your limitation. Your ability to get things done, to push and drive forward, to reach the result no matter what the personal cost, is no longer serving you, your team, or the organization as a whole. The rush of being the hero is not worth it. Or, better said, the rush of being that kind of short-term hero isn't worth it. Because when you help someone grow, and get beyond something that's been holding them back for years, that's heroic in a way. It's just a quiet way, one that won't get you in the papers but, if you're anything like me, will become the most meaningful part of your day.

And, on the flip side, these very qualities—your willpower and passionate care about getting great results—are the gift you can offer the people on your team. You do that by pulling back those qualities in yourself, to make room for them to step into their own versions. The waiting... is the hardest part. It won't happen overnight. They'll continue to expect you to jump in for a while, until you prove to them that you're strong enough to resist the urge.

If you need motivation, look carefully at the faces of the people on your team. Look beyond the friendly conversations, the small talk, and the status quo vibe. Can you see how drained people are, how hard they're working, and how much they're already holding? In your personal life, listen to the sighs of your loved ones as you utter words like "How do I get them to care as much as I do?" Your inner superhero, and I've never met a business leader who doesn't have one in some form, is the version of you that's standing between you and the dreams you want to reach.

Until I figured it out, I had no idea I was being Superman. I just thought I was doing my job. But I began to realize that the particular kind of superhero I embodied is one of three—the three archetypal leadership styles we'll turn to next. As you'll see, each one has a kind of strength run wild. By discovering your unique superhero style, and taking the risk to put the cape down, you'll be doing your part to transform your company culture, by making room for other people to grow beyond where they are today. It might just change their lives. It will definitely change yours.

CHAPTER TWELVE

Fixer, Fighter, or Friend?

Shake it off.
—Taylor Swift

Sometimes simply being in the room is a disempowering act. That's one of the hidden challenges of being in a leadership role. Whatever your background, there's an extremely high likelihood that the strength that got you this far has become a liability. For one thing, people are heavily conditioned to defer to authority. But there's another element that's far more within your control to address: When you're in charge, your opinion takes up more space than others', whether you intend it or not. What you say and do carries more weight. That's not necessarily a bad thing. It's only a bad thing when it's disempowering and demotivating others from finding their own voice.

In the last chapter you heard the story of how I discovered the Fighter archetype in myself. Perhaps you saw a bit of yourself in there. But there are two other archetypes that you might find closer to home, the Fixer and the Friend. Before we dive in, let's clarify our terms, specifically, why I'm choosing the word *archetype*. It has several meanings but the one I'm referring to is this one: a collectively inherited, unconscious idea, pattern of thought, image, etc., that is universally present in different individuals.

What I love about the word is that it's both solid and flexible at the same time. It describes something that is tangible, fixed enough to talk about in a way that makes sense. But, at the same time, archetypes have a flexibility to them, we can move between them, perhaps find ourselves in more than one. Most importantly, archetypes have shadow and light qualities. Each one contains a gift as well as a challenge created by that gift, which we must remain vigilant about.

You can use these archetypes in more than one way. You can, hopefully, find that your own dominant leadership style is one more than the other two. (For example, over the course of my career I've occupied the role of Fixer and Friend at times, but the Fighter is my go-to theme.) If you're a manager, these archetypes can also be a helpful lens through which to look at your team, or your organization as a whole. You might decide that you have a Fixer culture, which will inform what kinds of culture-wide communication and behavior you focus on changing. Since we've talked about the Fighter already, let's start with the Friend and work our way back.

The Friend

The Friend's motto: "We're all on the same team."

The Friend is the leader with the open door and a smile on their face. Remember Marcus from Chapter Seven? He showed us a great example of the strengths, weaknesses, and the transformative journey of the Friend. Friends are always available to answer questions, to offer encouragement to someone who's down, and try to treat each person on their team like they're a member of the family. Generally speaking, they're nice to be around, and once a cultural issue is brought to their attention, they spring into action to make things better. They care deeply about the experience their team is having. In many ways, of the three archetypes, Friends have the most natural skill when it comes to creating the kind of personal culture that you've been learning about in this book. When it comes to the care side of the equation, Friends have plenty in reserve. But this overflowing capacity for caring and generosity tends to backfire on Friends in the long run.

What Friend leaders don't often see is how fraught with risk it is to talk about how we're all in it together, or to say, as Friends often do, that the members of the team are all part of one big family. It's a noble wish to want to create a warm, personal, and welcoming vibe where people feel like they belong. But the word *family* is more than a little bit tricky for most people. It evokes at least as much difficult emotion as it does positive. And it sets up a very confusing mixed reality because you can't fire a member of your family, but you absolutely have to be able to fire someone who works for you who isn't pulling their weight. That doesn't mean don't ever work with family or close friends. But it does make things harder when it comes to employees feeling that accountability is for everyone and applied even-handedly. The closer you are to someone person-ally, *the higher the standard you have to hold them too*, to offset the natural tendency to give them the benefit of the doubt in a way that's unfair to others.

That leads us to the shadow side of Friend leadership: Friends struggle to hold a consistent standard of excellence. For obvious reasons, when push comes to shove and Friends have to choose between being tough and being nice, they'll tend to choose the nice option. This has serious ramifications for both the individ-uals on the team and the culture as a whole. Individuals tend not to get the kind of firm and clear boundaries they need to learn about themselves. As for teams, undue pressure is put on the stronger members to pick up the slack that results from the Friend being too lenient on the people who need some pressure. And those stronger players may resort to judging themselves, thinking along the lines of "Maybe I'm just being too hard on Chris, I mean the boss doesn't seem to think it's a problem." That internal dialogue that each person generates, trying to sort out what they're observing and how they feel about it— multiplied across the organization—is what creates the under-lying dynamics of a company culture. By being too nice, too accommodating, and too willing to look the other way, Friends will tend to create and support cultural dynamics that lack accountability and clear expectations around performance.

There's also a counterintuitive thing that happens often in Friend-led cultures. As a result of the lax standards and agree-ments around accountability, the problems that aren't being talked about need a place to go. This leads to gossip and poli-tics, often just below the surface of what looks like a happy and positive culture. People have a hard time being honest with each other because the culture mandates harmony over honesty. Even people who have strong opinions in other parts of their lives will adapt to the cultural mandate out of self-preservation. Better that than to risk being judged or criticized as "too intense." When the conversation can't be real, everybody loses.

As with the other two leadership archetypes, the Friend takes on too much responsibility for creating the vibe, worries about how others feel, and goes over the top to portray things in a positive and collegial way. The task for Friends is to pull back on that tendency and to do less active culture- and team-building themselves. With what you've already learned about strengths and weaknesses, you've probably made the connection. By shifting their focus, *by pulling back on their strengths and the micro-behaviors that they're used to relying on,* Friends open up space for others to take on some of those strengths and behaviors for themselves. And let's be clear: This pivot is not an easy one to make.

To create the culture they want, Friends have to deal with a fear, which we all have of course, but which drives Friends more than it does the other archetypes: the fear of not being liked. Friends have to be willing to accept the simple, uncomfortable truth: When you have people's paychecks in your hands, you don't get to be one of the gang. That's the price of leadership. When you do accept that reality, something very interesting can happen. Your team, feeling your clarity and purpose around the business, has the space to grow and change in the ways they're looking for as well. Friends can discover a new kind of professional relationship as a result, not as friendly or casual as before but far more alive and rewarding.

Let's summarize the Friend leadership archetype and outline their unique journey from Superman to Yoda:

The Friend's Gift. Friends have a natural care for people and don't need anyone to tell them about the importance of focusing on culture. They're service-oriented, often have deep religious or spiritual convictions, and will be the first to say "Culture is everything." Friends value human relationships and picking up someone up when they're down. Friends believe everyone deserves a second chance and have the heart to give it to them.

The Friend's Challenge. Friends struggle with creating a culture of accountability. Their worst nightmare is to be seen as a tyrant. Their compassion for people makes it hard to impose what feel like harsh consequences, even when they aren't in reality. In their reluctance to be seen as the bad guy (male or female), Friends deprive their team of one of the key elements of Good Authority: being willing to stand for the thing that needs to change and requiring each team member to do their own personal work to change it.

The Friend's Journey. To inhabit their strengths fully, Friends need to do some work to deepen their relationships outside of work, so that they need less friendship from the people on their team and are better able to tolerate the inevitable loneliness that comes with being in a leadership position, especially if they find themselves in the role of CEO. To reset the accountability dynamic internally, Friends should have a level-setting conversation with each member of their team, to clarify goals, roles, and responsibilities. And, crucially for all leaders who are learning about themselves, Friends must take 100 percent ownership for the dynamic they've created up to this point. You earn the right to ask people to adapt to a new agreement by acknowledging your role in creating and perpetuating the old one.

The Friend's Yoda Moment. Friend types are usually strong and self-deprecating communicators, they know how to talk about important things in a way that's lighthearted and straightforward. Here's the kind of thing Friend leaders might say, in their own words of course, to restart the culture conversation:

"Hey, so you know me and how much I want this place to be great and for you guys to have fun here. But I'm really at a loss about what to do. It's just one example but we've gotten this specific service complaint three times now, and I feel like nobody is really taking it seriously or taking responsibility for looking into why it's happening so we can do something about it. Fun is great, but it has to be a byproduct of doing great work, do you know what I mean?

How Can You Help a Friend? If you're a coach, consultant, or mentor to a Friend-type leader, the best way you can help is by holding them accountable for accepting the reality that it's lonely at the top—whether that's in the CEO seat or as a leader of a team within a larger organization. They'll need you to point out specific examples of how they've gotten too close to the people on their team, whether that's the tendency to be in too many meetings, the tone of their voice, or the way they socialize with people on the team. In the age of social media, bosses should be especially careful of how boundaries can get blurred if they become friends with employees on Facebook and so on, which happens all too often. No example is too small. Help them discover the courage to lead from a healthy distance, and you'll help them get back on the road to creating the culture they really want.

A Final Thought for the Friend. Here's a piece of advice especially useful for Friends who are taking over a new team or starting a new business, though it's worth keeping in mind regardless of your leadership style: There's no harm in starting out a little bit on the cool side, a little more formal and businesslike than you may want to be down the road. It's easier to warm up and become more vulnerable and transparent in your style over time. It's harder to go the other way, to reclaim the solid ground of authority you need once you've made yourself too much a part of the team at the outset.

The Fighter

The Fighter's motto: "Why wouldn't we?"

The Fighter is the leader with an overflowing cup of new ideas. And that's not restricted to the obvious things like inventing a new product or renaming the company. Fighters see ideas—i.e., opportunities for improvement—in every corner, from refinements to the business model, to small tweaks of existing products and processes, to the micro-moments on the customer journey. Fighters live in the truth that no matter what it is, it can always get better, you can always get a notch closer to the goal. The Fighter sees their business the way Michelangelo saw his famous statue: They have to remove every bit of stone that isn't *David*.

That is why working for a Fighter can be so enlivening. Fighters are the most naturally inspiring of the three archetypes: Their teams and organizations have purpose; they're going somewhere. If you work for a Fighter you feel like great work and innovative ideas matter. Fighters see opportunity and possibility at every turn. But, at some point, even though the Fighter may not run out of energy, the team will.

The shadow side of the Fighter is that they're hard to keep up with or compete with. It's not because they're faster or smarter than the other types, it's because they don't appreciate how much work they are creating in their wake. They don't realize how much space their ideas take up, leaving less room for the ideas of others. Fighters don't see how much they disempower their teams with their very presence. What Friends do by taking too much responsibility for being the social glue, Fighters do by taking too much responsibility for coming up with ideas. When a leader is so quick with ideas there's less motivation for the team to come up with their own ideas. And even if they do, on a Fighter-led team they won't have time to do anything with them.

New ideas take a lot of work to implement, and Fighters don't appreciate how that extra work affects people and takes them away from other, equally important, responsibilities. This work-creation element was off my radar as a Fighter-type leader for most of my career. I didn't realize that one idea from the CEO can easily create five projects, draw a dozen people into the loop, and drag them away from other priorities. Not to mention the very real cost of all that extra task-switching that's already out of control in the modern office.

Here's the irony: When Fighters learn to see these impacts and refine their approach by listening carefully to others, they get to see their two or three best ideas followed through on, as opposed to seeing their six or seven ideas all remaining in half-finished form. But the self-discipline to slow down has to come first. Being acknowledged and valued for coming up with ideas over a lifetime, Fighters rarely encounter someone who is strong enough to hold them accountable for reigning in their creativity. I was fortunate enough to have a mentor do that for me at a critical moment in my career, as I shared in Chapter Eight.

There are two ways in which Fighters typically don't follow through. First, they generate ideas and tend not to complete them. While the Fighter has moved on to the next idea, the next great adventure or new technology, the team is left holding the bag. This causes frustration for the team, and over the long haul undermines the inspirational and motivational qualities the Fighter otherwise brings to the table. Second, Fighters rarely get to the post-game analysis. Even when their ideas do get implemented, they don't pause to understand and quantify the results, so those results do not inform subsequent ideas they generate, which leads to more wasted effort, and on and on.

The Fighter's Gift. Fighters never stop asking why. They're always pushing for things to get better. They're naturally inspiring, often idealistic, and have a knack for seeing potential in others that they don't see in themselves. They're driven by a desire to make the world a better place.

The Fighter's Challenge. Fighters struggle to see the value of the little things. They're reluctant to go to the next decimal point, to track projects down to their real costs in time, money, and morale, because they don't want to be sidetracked from implementing their next idea. The Fighter's worst nightmare is the status quo.

The Fighter's Journey. The transformative moment for Fighters is to accept the world as it is, and learn that change happens with small steps and ongoing refinement. They need to build up the muscle of going to that next decimal point, to see that doing so doesn't take away creativity or self-expression but rather liberates it. They will initially see deadlines, limited resources, and existing inefficiencies as lumps of coal, but as they make the pivot, Fighters will begin to see them as the source of the diamonds within.

The Fighter's First Step. For most Fighters the first step is to clean up the past with their team, to acknowledge the toll that their style has taken to date, and to be willing to see how overwhelmed everyone has become. It might sound like this:

"Hey, guys, I've been doing some thinking and I realize how fast I've been going, how hard I've been pushing you. I didn't see it till now. I'm really sorry. I know some of you have tried to tell me and I wasn't listening. I'd really like to turn that around and I'd love your ideas for how to do that. One idea that I had, I promise it's not more work, is for us all to get together and figure out which projects we can archive, which ideas we can delete, and so on, to clean out all of our inboxes and make more space for the right things to get the attention they deserve. How does that sound?"

How Can You Help a Fighter? The best gift you can give a Fighter is a strong accountability partner. That could be a manager strong on data-driven process and improvement, a strong-minded coach or mentor who will push back when their minds wander. Whoever it is they have to be someone who can meet and match the Fighters' energy, who can build trust and then show the Fighter how to redirect that energy more effectively. Hold them accountable to pull back, and to keep pulling back, until others start to emerge with ideas and initiatives of their own. In this way you will help Fighters achieve their dream: to build a team driven by ideas and not afraid to risk the unknown on the road to creating something great.

A Final Word for the Fighter. Granularity is your new best friend. Take the time to break down problems into their component parts. Then break the components down into their parts, and look for the patterns and connections between them. What if you change the sequence? What if you took out step three entirely? The smaller you're willing to get, the more power your ideas will have in the end.

The Fixer

The Fixer's motto: *"If you want it done right, you have to do it yourself."*

The Fixer is the archetype that will sound most familiar. I've left Fixers until last because of all that's been written about them over the years. They're the most misunderstood of the three—the leaders and managers who tend to the micromanagement side of life, who live in the world of tasks, crossing things off the list, catching others' mistakes and their own. Fixers check everything personally before it goes out the door. They spend their days polishing things until they're perfect, and are finely attuned to the little problems that are coming down the pike that others will tend to brush off. Fixers fix whatever they can find that's broken. That gift, once unleashed, is the leadership path for the Fixer. Because of the skill and attention to detail that comes naturally to them more than to the other two types, Fixers can become the embodiment of excellence. That is, once they get out of the way of excellence in others.

There's a question I used to ask to flush out the Fixers in an audience of leaders. "Don't you just hate how you have to jump in and fix problems for your team, how if you don't get in there and do it, it won't get done right?" The Fixers will reveal themselves instantly (though not after they read this!) with a knowing groan or woe-is-me sigh that says, "Don't I know it … If only I could find good people who cared about excellence as much as I do."

"Liars, all of you!" I would say, playfully of course. "You love being the hero! You love jumping in and saving the day." Then knowing laughter fills the room, the laughter of allowing ourselves to be seen and feeling liberated by it. Fixers feel better in the act of fixing. It scratches an itch, it makes them feel valued, important, and useful. The pivot for Fixers is to see how much they're filling the space, in the same way Fighters and Friends do in their ways. Except instead of trying to be the social glue or the idea glue, Fixers try to hold things together with excellence glue. But their standards are so high that, over time, the rest of the team will give up on even trying to reach them.

The Fixer's Gift. Fixers are consummate professionals, artisans in their chosen craft. They take the time to do it right. At their best, they invest in the last centimeter of the customer experience, or in a moment of mentoring to take the time to fully explain what they mean, because that's what care looks like to them. They're delighted by subtle experiences and make a point of delivering that kind of delight to others. They have the capacity—though they often have to learn the patience—to mentor, train, and challenge people to a standard of excellence that is greatly sought after in our world.

The Fixer's Challenge. The flipside of this standard of care is that Fixers often lose the forest for the trees. They're so busy fixing typos, calling back disgruntled customers, and double-checking everything that they have trouble zooming out and putting themselves in the shoes of someone who is going through something that they don't understand or haven't experienced themselves. When they're not vigilant, Fixers' desire for control and order blinds them to the messier, more personal, and more human elements of leading a team.

The Fixer's Journey. Fixers transform their leadership style by learning to let go of the need for too much control. Instead of learning to let go of being the one with ideas, or being the one who cheers people up, they need to let go of being the one in charge of company-wide quality control.

The Fixer's First Step. To begin their journey from Superman to Yoda, Fixers need new experiences. They'll benefit more than the other two types from time outside the office, retreats of any kind, structured or not. The path of Fixers is to fall back into themselves, to take a two-week cell-phone-free vacation, to indulge themselves in what will feel like reckless amounts of self-care, a massage after work before coming home for dinner. Here's a declaration a Fixer might make when they're ready to change things:

"So, I'll be out next month for a few weeks. Let's spend some time making sure you guys have everything you need before I go, because I won't be taking my phone with me. I'm not going to lie, this is going to be hard for me, but I want to take a step to show you how much I mean what I say... that I trust you to take care of things in my absence. You guys have great judgment, better than I give you credit for sometimes. And this is one small step in the direction of making some more room around here."

How Can You Help a Fixer? Fixers need to be held accountable for strategic thinking. If you manage or coach a Fixer, it will often feel like you're having to pull their fingers off the steering wheel one by one. Do it with a smile on your face and keep it light-hearted. Each time you do, let them know why, and make sure to remind them whose job it is to do the thing they were about to do themselves. Keep reminding them that each step they take away from fixing is a step closer to leading. They'll thank you for it in the end.

A Final Word for the Fixer. Don't look. As hard as it will be at first, find opportunities to not look at other people's work. Ask to be removed from the cc field on email threads. Encourage your team to use each other for a second look on things instead of coming to you. Bow out of meetings that are about process or implementation. Make yourself available for the big picture stuff. Don't fall into the trap of thinking that you'll have time for strategic work and big picture thinking when you're done checking off your list.

Whichever of the leadership archetypes best fits you—Fixer, Fighter, or Friend—don't use it as a tool to self-criticize, though who doesn't benefit from a little light-hearted teasing coming from people who love them? As you think about these ideas in the days ahead, remember that leadership is not a destination: It's a process. It's each of us learning a little bit more each day about who we are, who we want to be tomorrow, and what we can do today to get a little bit closer. And if you're ever in doubt—whether you're a Fixer, Fighter, or a Friend—less is almost always more.

CHAPTER THIRTEEN

THE FIVE EMPLOYEE ARCHETYPES

_Our strengths are not our own until they are freed
of the burden of having to heal the past._

It's not something we normally think about it, but there are
only three kinds of relationships that exist between any two
people in an organization. If you take a mental snapshot of
everyone at your office, you'll see that: (1) they report to you,
(2) you report to them, or (3) you are peers (neither of you has
authority over the other). I'd love to see us teach kids some of
these basic authority dynamics in high school, why we relate
to different people differently based on their roles, and how to
question authority respectfully, because so many of the problems that exist in the modern workplace stem from a basic

misunderstanding of how to relate with authority in a healthy way. That healthy way, simply put, consists of the ability to stand for yourself and express what you feel in a way that honors the current agreement between you.

As we saw in our discussion of the Friend archetype, many leaders are trying to flatten the hierarchy of their organizations via shared office space, "we're all on the same team" messages, and so on. They're not accepting, and so can't work with, the reality that when you're the boss you can never not be the boss. On the flipside, many employees don't know how to relate with a boss from their own self-authority, to stand for what they feel without going over the line. As an employee, no matter how passionate you are about your viewpoint, you have to accept that your boss has anxieties and concerns that you don't, and is also very likely to be looking at a different set of data than you are.

It's worth taking the time to inventory your professional relationships and ask yourself questions like "In which relationships am I the boss but not really acting like one?"; "In which relationships am I the subordinate but not acting like one?"; and "In which relationships am I a peer but acting like either a boss or a subordinate?" Learning to appreciate and acknowledge the hierarchical structure of each relationship doesn't undermine creativity and individuality, it allows the space for it, because then people are freed up to speak their mind without trying to navigate hidden or subtle organizational politics. A clear and current organizational chart, with some discussion, can clear up far more of the culture challenge than you might think.

It's within these dynamics—in particular between manager and direct employee and vice-versa—where all of the good stuff is. The direct management relationship is the most intense, challenging, and professionally intimate—intimate in the sense that your manager gets to know your habits and quirks in a way few other people in your life ever do. And if you're anywhere in the potentially vast middle of the org chart, if you're anywhere other than the CEO position or a frontline one, you have both dynamics going on at once, many times over. More than one person is your boss and you are the boss of more than one person. To make matters more complex, with your co-managers you have peer relationships, which have their own potential pitfalls and, of course, wonderful upsides as well.

In short, a manager inhabits the most interpersonally complex role in a modern organization, in many ways more complex than the CEO role. Which is why this chapter is especially relevant for managers and team leaders. Everyone can benefit from looking into whether they're a Fixer, Fighter, or Friend, as we did in the last chapter. But the five employee archetypes you'll learn about next will help you mentor each person on your team with even greater specificity and reach more profound professional and personal results.

Before we proceed, I want to share two fears that I have. My first fear—why I went back and forth on whether to include this chapter and "Fixer, Fighter, or Friend?"—was introducing a personality typing system that people might use to categorize and dehumanize others, as I've seen happen with so many other tools of this kind. My hope is you'll use this as a resource to assist in the personal growth of the people on your team—and, of course, to help yourself as well. In other words, be careful not to confuse the map for the territory. In the end, I've decided to include both chapters, with this caveat: Please use the ideas in this chapter with the utmost of care. Feel free to email me and ask for help with how to apply them.

My second fear is oversimplifying something that is actually quite complex. The complexity takes two forms. First, you may discover that people on your team don't fall neatly into one of the five archetypes—just as most leaders aren't *only* Fixers, Fighters, or Friends. Use whatever aspects of these tools serve you, and leave the rest. Trust that if you let go of an important element now, it will come back to you later, as you need it. The second form of complexity is the interrelationship between the two systems. For example, as a team leader you might discover that the Fixer pattern best describes you, but in your relationship with your boss, you play the role of the Provocateur. So which archetype is going to help you grow at work? Use Fixer, Fighter, or Friend when you're working on yourself as a leader, and use the Five Employee Archetypes when you're looking across the table at the people who report to you. Fixer, Fighter, and Friend are about how you relate to *being* an authority. The Five Archetypes are about how you relate to *having* an authority.

The Five Archetypes

Accountability is a personal process. There's a thin line between being a helpful mentor and pushing someone beyond the growth they're ready for today (which can be very different tomorrow). When you add the baggage we all carry about relating with authority figures, it's reasonable to want to run the other way and leave employee development to someone else. The Five Employee Archetypes are designed to give you a framework to think about it differently. You'll learn to hold each member of your team accountable for growth in a way that's far more about drawing them out into their strengths than harping on their weaknesses.

Each person on your team comes to the office with a unique personal history, deeply held values, personal pains, and of course, hopes and dreams. Without filing down anyone's specific, beautiful humanness, over the years I've seen five behavior patterns emerge. Each one of these is a composite of different people I've met over the course of my career—people who've worked for me, who I've worked for, and who I've worked alongside of—and they're informed by the managers and CEOs I've worked with as a mentor and coach along the way as well.

As you read through the archetypes, try and find yourself. Without pigeonholing anyone too quickly, see which archetype reminds you of each person on your team. Think about your boss too, and maybe even people in your personal life. The broader your perspective, the more likely you'll be able to apply the archetypes with compassion and care, and to approach them with a willingness to meet people where they are. That is the only place from which we can all grow, and suffer the least amount of slipping back into old patterns.

The Pragmatist

None of the patterns are better or worse than any other, but Pragmatists generally have an easier time than most being challenged by their managers. They've decided, based on their own personal experience, that there's nothing inherently untrustworthy about authority. They likely have already had strong mentoring figures in their lives, perhaps a parent who had the knack for encouraging them in just the right way.

Pragmatists' strength is in being able to execute on ideas and projects without unnecessary drama. They know how to put their heads down and get things done. They're organized. They tend to be considerate of the feelings and challenges of their teammates. They look for compromises and enjoy working with different kinds of people. They're especially fond of creative types. They're inspired by the risks creative people take and see more of who they want to be in them. They know that they can help the creative type get grounded with their ideas and make them more real, more quickly.

The Pragmatists' challenge, as you'll see emerge with each of the archetypes, is in the mirror image of the dynamic they're comfortable with. In their willingness to work it out, to make space for others, and to find a way through that works for everyone, Pragmatists will tend to minimize the value of their own voice. They're more likely to hang back in a team meeting, to listen rather than interject, an admirable quality that can also be hugely limiting. They tend to not push back hard enough against the ideas and initiatives of the people in authority when they disagree with them, and let their silence build up as resentment over time. They see flaws in logic, inefficiencies and, often secretly, they have very strong and valuable ideas about how things could be done differently. But they keep it to themselves.

The best way to help Pragmatists is to challenge them to own this hidden strength. While it might not sound like accountability, the way to help people who tend to this pattern is to stop validating them for the things they're already great at. They don't need more praise about their timeliness, willingness to collaborate, and professionalism. They need praise for the moments when they break out of their shell, when they speak up with half-formed thoughts instead of waiting to have it all sorted. They'll need your help as their manager (or mentor, etc.) to push them to do this, as they won't see the value of it until much later.

Give them assignments to stretch their creative mind. Force them to delegate running a meeting to someone else so they're not busy administering things. Give them a goal of sharing three half-formed ideas in every meeting for the next month. Hold them accountable for taking a half-day a week outside the office to work on a creative project they've been delaying, to come up with a new product idea without doing any new research, to go to a networking or industry event. Perhaps you could even have them write a post for the company blog about how to make space for creative time—so they have to teach what they need to learn!

In short, help Pragmatists unlock their creative side by holding them accountable for not over-relying on the strength they already have, the one that has gotten them this far. They'll never lose the practical side, it's not in their DNA to be sloppy or disorganized. They won't fritter a day away in idea-generating mode—but wouldn't it be incredible for your team if they did?

The Provocateur

You've probably come across Provocateurs more than once in your career. They're the team members who push the envelope, who are never satisfied with the current plan or direction, who are sure they have a better idea. They often do. The problem is that they don't yet have the skills to manage their ideas without driving their teammates crazy. In contrast to Pragmatists, they tend to take too many risks without thinking through the consequences, and they often fall short of the mark when it comes to communicating with their teammates. Remember Cheryl from back in Chapter Four? She was a great example of a Provocateur in light and shadow, and the mentoring path we took together is a model of how you can help them grow.

As with all of the archetypes, there will be clues to Provocateurs in their early authority relationships, whether you know anything about them or not. They likely had at least one parent who was deeply supportive of their creative side, perhaps encouraged them in music, the arts, or even as they buried themselves in their rooms as teenagers, coding away on their laptop. They were valued as creative beings, perhaps more so than the other archetypes. And, as with the other archetypes, this strength gets in their way. People who fit this archetype often struggle with boundaries, when to turn the creative engine off and commit to a deadline, to call a project good enough, to analyze the results of their work in depth before moving on to the next thing.

The best way you can help Provocateurs grow is to set clear boundaries. Hold them accountable for deadlines, for detailed communication, for staying on top of their commitments. As you do that, remember to acknowledge the small things they do along the way to improve, especially in their relationships with their teammates. You'll help the Provocateur find a frame for their incredible creativity to flourish in more productive ways. They'll develop strategies to bring their teammates with them. Recognizing they are part of a team of people who have gifts that complement their own will help Provocateurs feel a little bit less alone.

Because they're not used to being held accountable for the details, Provocateurs can be the most difficult of the archetypes to mentor. You'll find yourself having to be the bad guy. You may feel like you're squashing their creativity and being the worst kind of cold-hearted bureaucrat. You're not. What you're doing, if you take up the challenge to help Provocateurs grow, is giving them a kind of strength that they don't yet have. The more creative force a person has, the more they need boundaries and a container from which that creativity can emerge. They may kick and scream for a while, as this self-admitted Provocateur has done more than once in his career, but they will never forget the gift you've given them.

The Protector

We all struggle with how to bring what we feel into our professional lives, but this struggle is what defines the Protector. Protectors are highly sensitive humans, deeply attuned to their inner world and to the inner worlds of others. They can be highly empathic and great team players. They generally light up the room that they're in. Whenever I think about the Protector I think about Victoria. Victoria worked in regulatory affairs for a clean energy venture that I'd cofounded back in the early 2000s. Her role was to oversee the complex pool of stakeholders (government agencies, transmission planning committees, community groups, etc.) that we were in constant communication with over the multi-year process of getting permission to break ground on our projects. She mostly made it look easy, sifting through the byzantine regulations as if it were just any old thing. She was quick with a smile and I never heard anyone say an unkind word about her.

The challenge with Victoria was in her private life, which would normally have been none of my business, but which had become an emotional roller coaster that was affecting her work. It didn't surface until about a year in, but in a series of conversations when things started to get bumpy she confided in me that her brother was in and out of rehab, that her parents had retired and her father was struggling with his health, and that it was all getting to her, far more than she wanted to admit to herself.

The problem wasn't that these things were going on for Victoria, but that they had started to affect her work. It began with a few careless mistakes on a key application filing. Last-minute emergencies caused her to miss a handful of regulatory meetings that weren't mandatory for us but would certainly have helped our cause. The straw that broke the camel's back was an email standoff she got into about one of our projects with an influential member of the local community who was, admittedly, being a jerk. I knew then that I had to intervene.

What Victoria needed, what Protectors need, is room to feel what they feel. They need someone—and it doesn't have to be their manager—to let them know that it's okay to be going through a rough time at home and still come to work. In fact, coming to work could be the best thing for a personal rough patch, as long as the person can develop some skills around dealing with raw emotions while on the clock. Protectors' relationship to early authority is worth talking a bit about here. The reason they keep things bottled up the way they do is because, for whatever reason, they were often the person in their family who did just that. They held the emotions for other people and smoothed the waters, but forgot about themselves too much along the way. This is what made Victoria great at her job in one way, but also what started to take it off the rails when she reached her limit.

The best way to support the growth of someone who you feel fits the Protector archetype is to find ways to make it safe for them to bring more of who they are to the office. It might start out just with you. This is true for everyone, but especially for Protectors: You can give them an incredible gift just by noticing that they're having a rough week and saying something. "Hey, seems like you've got a lot going on right now. Just want you to know it's fine and I'm here if you need anything." In the right moment, you can challenge Protectors to be a little more transparent with the team, not about the precise content of what's going on but about the general outlines. "Hey guys, just so you know, I'm going through a rough patch with some stuff outside of work. My brother just went back into rehab on Sunday so I may be a bit distracted this week. Maybe it'll be fine, but I just wanted you to know."

As I've seen too many times to remember in my life and in the lives of others, when Victoria opened up in this small but nevertheless completely vulnerable way, especially given who she was, the team rallied around her. More than one person went to her proactively seeing what they could take off her plate that week, or maybe just had a second thought about including her on an email thread that she didn't need to be on. In our individual meetings, I saw my role as making space for whatever came up around it all. Sometimes she'd volunteer a bit of how things were progressing outside of work, in general terms. Sometimes, when I knew she wouldn't volunteer it, I'd ask, just to make sure she knew it was okay and that having struggles outside of work wasn't something she had to fix.

Once Victoria was able to remain open to the reality that our emotions don't disappear when we walk through the office door, things were fine. She had an outlet for what was going on, so it didn't come out sideways in the course of her work.

Being vulnerable at work doesn't mean expressing your emotions outwardly all the time. In fact, it usually means being able to share transparently what is going on for you *instead of* wearing it on your sleeve and pretending it isn't there. It's the difference between, on the one hand, snapping at your teammates or being sarcastic throughout the day, and on the other, saying "Hey guys, I'm really frustrated about something right now. Has nothing to do with you guys, but if I'm a little extra edgy today please let me know so I can stop it." Emotional transparency as opposed to emotional expression—saying what you feel instead of acting it out—is key to creating a healthy team and cultural dynamic. The emotion isn't unnecessary, only the drama is!

The mentoring journey with Protectors is to give them the experience that having emotions and being a professional are not two different things. They are one. When they integrate the richness of their emotional world, pain and all, Protectors get to be who they are and get a new gift from you and everyone else around them. Perhaps for the first time in their lives they don't have to hold it all by themselves. Can you imagine giving a gift like that to someone on your team?

The Peacemaker

Jesse worked in P.R. for a client I was working with a while back, a small but growing civil engineering firm based in Seattle. After a brief stint at a large agency, she'd made the jump to go in-house. She focused on helping the engineering firm increase their profile and their chances to win contracts on some larger and more lucrative projects. Jesse was a great example of the fourth employee archetype: the Peacemaker.

While I worked only briefly with Jesse directly, the theme that emerged in working with her manager over a longer period of time was consistent: She didn't know how to say "I don't know," and she especially didn't know how to say it when her boss was around. Initially her new team felt she was a godsend, someone who would take on everything that came her way and handle it. But, over time, the gaps started to show. She was taking things on but she wasn't really handling them. Not because she didn't want to, but because she was lacking in a skillset or a piece of background for that particular task. She didn't have the confidence to say, for example, "Yes, I'd be happy to. But one thing. It's a bit embarrassing given my background doing a lot of contracts and I know that's what you hired me for, but I've never actually negotiated one of these specific types of contracts before and I don't know the wrinkles. Is it okay if I come to you for a little more support than usual on this first one?" To avoid a potential conflict or embarrassment, Jesse pretended that she knew things she didn't. She defaulted to thinking that her value was in having the right answers instead of asking the right questions.

As the name evokes, perhaps the Peacemaker's early relationships with authority were characterized by more violence or aggression than the other types, and that informs the working style they've developed over the years. Whatever the cause, they've learned to master the art of getting through a conflict without further insult or injury. It's an admirable strength, being able to weather professional storms just as they do personal ones. But the overreliance on that strength comes at a cost. From the perspective of a manager, the challenge of having the Peacemaker on your team is that it's very hard to know where they stand. They make it hard for teammates in the same way. By being difficult to read, they put others in the position of worrying about upsetting them, or walking on eggshells. In the speed of the day, people will often work around Peacemakers because they can't trust that they'll ask questions about what they don't know.

Even though it is the furthest thing from their intention, Peacemakers will tend to introduce doubt and uncertainty into the minds of their managers and colleagues. It's not that they're not thinking, working hard, or being creative. It's that the elusiveness that characterizes them, often without them realizing, has the net effect of undermining people's trust in them. Perhaps ironically, Peacemakers can be the hardest of the five archetypes to help. Because peace—while it might sound good to some on the surface—is a goal that's anathema to a growing organization. A sense of calm and general order is one thing. But peace means no conflict. And no conflict in an organization is a very not-good thing.

The best way to help Peacemakers grow is to start a conversation with them about the pattern as gently as possible. Look for the tiniest grains of sand that you see the Peacemaker get frustrated or annoyed by and zoom in on them, to give your Peacemaker the experience that it's okay to be frustrated or annoyed, and more importantly, that it's okay to let others know how their actions are affecting the Peacemaker. Go slow. Walk them through the process you go through when you need to have a tough conversation with someone. Debrief it with them afterwards to give them the space to talk it out, to show them that healthy conflict leads to closeness and connection. Help them undo the story that's been holding them back for too long.

One exercise you can give to a Peacemaker—when they're ready and you've talked about it for a bit—is to have them create a list of the things that frustrate them and share it with the rest of the team. Peacemakers have huge insights into what's not quite right, and everyone wins if you find a way to draw that out of them. Ask them: "What are the top ten things that you don't like about working here, the things that we're not doing right for our customers, the things that we're missing opportunities on as a leadership team?" They'll need encouragement, but they'll secretly love the exercise, and the permission to stretch in a way they may never have done before.

The Performer

The last of the five archetypes is the Performer. Performers are the members of the team who excel at a particular skill. It could be more technical, like being fluent in a certain programming language, or more relationship-oriented, like knowing how to talk with a frustrated customer in a human way. Whatever their chosen specialty, Performers have gotten to where they are in their careers by honing and refining it. They have a focus and attention to detail that's greatly valued by employers, which helps Performers get and keep jobs, and keep business ventures afloat, throughout their careers.

The challenge for Performers lies in the dynamic nature of the modern workplace. In today's office, no matter what skill you have, that skill is morphing and changing in response to changing technology and a radically new set of customer expectations and experiences. Without learning to adapt, Performers run the risk of getting stuck in the way they've always done things. Under pressure, they double down on their skill instead of opening up to new experiences and knowledge. In a kind of paradox, Performers' biggest challenge is to not let their craftsmanship get in the way of picking their head up long enough and consistently enough to keep evolving.

Helping Performers to become more flexible and adaptive can have dramatic personal effects. I'm reminded of one man who was on a team of mine for a few years who fit the Performer mold, who through his evolution at work, rediscovered a sense of adventure that he had lost decades before. When you're as good at something as the Performer is, it's easy to feel that you don't belong, or that others don't get or appreciate your unique talent. Having a manager and mentor in your life who can see the world through your eyes can be life-changing.

As with the other archetypes, it's worth considering how early authority relationships may play into a Performer's pattern. They may have had a role model in one or both parents who excelled at a particular craft, a technical skill of one kind or another that served them well throughout their career and kept food on the table growing up. Alongside those positive messages may have come another one: Work that isn't in the realm of craftsmanship has less value. Early authority figures may have colored Performers' perceptions when it comes to the relationship side of business—in particular, collaboration with teammates, and compromises on how much resource can be dedicated to different parts of a job. Performers can see these kinds of things as politics and bureaucracy that are getting in the way of their craft, instead of a necessary part of building a great team and close professional relationships.

The best way to help Performers is to show them the personal price they're paying in keeping their distance from the team. Unlike Peacemakers and Protectors, who tend to be overly attuned to the inner worlds of others, Performers tend to not consider others nearly enough. Gently encourage Performers out of their solitary tendencies, and into the joys of working with others, by inviting them to participate in collaborative projects, or perhaps to lead a team meeting. Have them come up with ideas that other people do the technical work on, and you may just find a manager in the making: A Performer who learns how to open the space for others to do great work can become an exceptional team leader or executive.

As with all the tools and ideas in this book—including the Five Archetypes—experiment with them in the days and months ahead. Do talk about them with your team. Don't keep them a secret. If you have someone on your team who you think fits one of the descriptions, why not share it with them and find out what they think? Maybe there's another pattern that speaks to them more, or it leads to a conversation about something else entirely. By opening up the conversation in these ways you'll remove any unnecessary feelings of being categorized or judged, as can happen with personality tools and assessments. You may be surprised at how interested people are in their own growth. I've been shocked more than once in my career by seeing someone who I thought had no interest in learning about themselves turn out to be very insightful about their own growth, once I made it safe for them to talk about it.

A final thought. While the five employee archetypes and the three leadership archetypes can lead to important personal discoveries, your job is to focus on the discoveries that are relevant to work. Simply put: It's not your job to ask questions about the past or why someone learned to relate with authority the way they did. For you to make them feel even the least bit compelled to share that is out of bounds. It's also out of bounds for leaders and managers to overshare personal history and challenges outside of work. That would be a grave misunderstanding of what it means to be vulnerable and transparent in a leadership role. You model it all for your team by being real with what's true in your heart, and consciously choosing what's relevant and appropriate to say out loud. It's another way of making sure you don't take up too much space, and leave plenty of room for the challenges, growth, and dreams of each and every person on your team.

The bottom line: Keep it about the work and everything else will take care of itself. Get as specific as you can about how you're seeing their personal struggles affecting goals and metrics. That won't make your feedback cold and impersonal. It will help to ground it with real examples that people can relate to. How is their behavior making it harder for others to do their job? How is it frustrating a customer or requiring you to step in, which takes you away from the work you need to be doing? Last but not least, how are they holding themselves back by doing something that's taking them further away from their next promotion instead of closer to it?

Invest in the process of personal growth with each person and you'll create a rare and beautiful thing in our world: a team of people pursuing their individual self-interests in a way that contributes to the passionate pursuit of a collective goal. You'll foster that kind of team by being willing to get to know each of them and by letting them get to know you. You have the capacity to help them get closer to achieving their individual dreams through their work in your organization.

From there the task is simple but not easy. Keep your focus

and theirs not on checking tasks off of lists, but on finding root causes. Hold them accountable for personal behavior; don't let them indulge in excuses or blame the system. Show them how taking ownership of their work and taking ownership of their life are exactly the same thing.

CHAPTER FOURTEEN

PULL THE THREAD

Because things are the way they are,
things will not stay the way they are.
—Bertolt Brecht

We live in an interesting time. We're not the first generations to feel this way, but we are at a pivotal moment. It's not about the endless wars, that's unfortunately how it's always been. It's not about technology or social media, though clearly we have a lot more work to do to figure out how to relate with the tools we now have at hand in a way that makes us feel more humane and not less. And, as passionate as I feel about the subject of climate change, that's ultimately not what I think the pivot is about either. It's about the convergence of all of it, how all of these unstoppable forces are coming together to show us ourselves in a way that no sane person can ignore. We are being held accountable for our choices.

We are being invited to look in the mirror, to stop our self-destructive patterns, and we're being shown the consequences of not doing so. You could see that as depressing and give up hope. Or you could see it as the greatest gift and challenge there is. How do we adapt to this radically faster and exponentially more connected world, and do it in a way where we're decreasing our footprint on the planet at the same time? It's a challenge that will require the best from us—as many of us as possible, as fast as we can. Which brings us to a paradox.

The paradox is contained in that word: *change*. The word has been woven throughout this book but we haven't yet talked about it specifically. It's one of the tricky ones, one of those words that we often assume we share a definition of but don't. But there's one feeling that most of us have about change that we hold onto pretty stubbornly even though we know better. We want change to happen fast. It doesn't—not the kind of personal change we've talked about in this book. But wanting change to go fast is not the problem. The problem is *why* we want it to go fast. We think of change as a destination we have to get to, in order to become our better selves, when really it's an ongoing process, which we can learn to dance with, which, over time, can allow us to become our better selves. Change is not where we're going, it's who we are.

When we actually make a change, we often have the odd feeling of "That's it? That's all there was to it?" That's because, in that moment, we've overcome resistance to being with change itself. The new thing we're doing or way we're being often isn't that big a deal, and isn't the hard part. The hard part is the willingness to let go of the past, especially when we've fooled ourselves into thinking that we already have. Change isn't uncomfortable, but the prospect of changing is. By definition, change is not what we're used to. It doesn't give us the sense of solidity, the sense of certainty and control that we're accustomed to. And right there, in the clinging to certainty and familiarity, lies the opportunity to lean into the most difficult, most rewarding aspect of being alive: learning to be okay with not knowing.

We spend our lives running in the other direction, feeling like we have or need the answers, that we know or want to know where we're going and exactly how long it's going to take to get there. We strive in big ways and small to give ourselves just a little bit more of that feeling of certainty any chance we get. Which makes the irony that much more thick, because when we find even the least bit of comfort with the unknown, on a walk in the woods, or sitting quietly with a cup of coffee on Saturday morning while the kids are still in bed, what happens? We relax. We exhale. We smile in the knowing that yes, of course, that is how it's always been. That is us. This is life. We are characters in the greatest mystery story ever told, a story that is still being written.

When we let ourselves not have the answer we feel more like ourselves, because we are being honest. By not having the answer we open up to the source of all creativity and innovation. The more comfortable we can get with it, the more we can get in relationship with it instead of pretending we've got it handled, the better things get. We don't only become more inspired or more productive. We become more of ourselves. Only then can the leader within each one of us emerge, naturally, without too much force or too much fear, just you, saying what you think, feeling what you feel, and doing what you know is the right thing to do.

That's the choice you have each and every day when you go to work. Whether you just graduated from school last week, or have been the CEO of a multinational corporation for the last 25 years. You can choose wonder over certainty, now instead of later, and see fear not as a reason to shut down but as a reminder to open up.

I hope this book has inspired you with some new ideas and things to try, and will challenge you to become a Good Authority to the people in your world. Whether you lead a team of three, are a CEO of ten thousand, or are the parent of one. True leadership is a gift that gives both ways: You become more of who you are by helping others do the same. You do it by meeting each person where they are, pushing them to go just a little bit further, and letting them know that you'll be there when they fall. Not to catch them and tell them not to feel bad. But to help them figure out why they did, to steady themselves and to give it another go. And then, when they're ready, when they take the leap and realize they had it in themselves all along, you can rest and celebrate as they do.

And when the moment has passed, take a walk down the hall … see who's around … and start all over again.

A FINAL THOUGHT

The notion of "work–life balance" has always bugged me. I think it's what was behind a phone call I made to my parents all the way back in 1994. I was approaching the end of my senior year in college, and I swore to my parents that I would never have a nine-to-five job. I've broken that promise for the better part of the twenty years since. But "work–life balance" never stopped bugging me. I've never been able to swallow what feels like a big dose of resignation embedded in it. Maybe that resignation is hiding behind the dash. I've always wanted to live in a world where my work and my life were not two things, but one. And if you've made it this far, I'm sure you feel the same way.

I'm far from a workaholic. I take a nap every afternoon and will jump at any chance I can to get on a paddleboard in a warm ocean and watch the sea turtles float by below. I don't think we should live to work. But "work to live" doesn't capture it either. Where we all want to be is somewhere right in the middle. It's hard to describe but unmistakable when we find it. It's in the moments when we lose ourselves in our passion, when the hours go by too fast, when doing what we do leaves us feeling like we are becoming more of who we are.

I've spent the last twenty years, my whole life in many ways, trying to find that sweet spot for myself. There have been many rough patches along the way. It took me a long time to accept that the rough patches are the price of admission to a meaningful life. That the work of staying true to our values is a lot trickier than it sounds.

Who I am is everything I've learned. I am all the mistakes I've ever made. I am my greatest successes and joys. And I've had many mentors along the way—some loud ones, some quiet ones, some who didn't even know my name. Because of them, I'm standing here today, writing to you about what Good Authority is and how it can help you achieve your dreams. Because it—because they—have helped me to achieve mine.

My deepest hope is that the ideas in this book can contribute to a new conversation that will fulfill the promise, the one that is in the air as I write these words in the spring of 2016, that the world of work can become a source of joy, of personal connection and meaning for far more people than it is today. That, together, we create a new standard for what we expect from the authorities in our world, at work, at home, and beyond. Ultimately, I hope this book helps two people somewhere sit down across from each other and have a little bit easier time talking about something that's been on their minds.

Please let me know if there's anything I can do to help.

ACKNOWLEDGEMENTS

As a first-time author, I didn't know how intimate a process it was going to be to write this book and put it out into the world. And how important it is to name names of the people who helped to give it life. Thanks to my wife, Aleks, for sharing your boundless heart with me; my daughter Livia, for making the world better every time you smile; my publisher Rohit Bhargava for taking a shot on a first-time author; my editor Matthew Sharpe for believing in this book from the first draft and lovingly guiding me through every step; my friends Rick Snyder and Tiffany Lach for your invaluable feedback on the early drafts; my parents, Steve and Beth, for your generous and forgiving hearts; and last but not least, to my friend Bernadette Jiwa, who held me accountable for three years with one simple question: "So, Jonathan, when are you going to write your book?"

ABOUT THE AUTHOR

After twenty years of not being able to decide whether he was a business development guy or a personal growth teacher, Jonathan stopped trying to figure it out. These days you'll find him at refound.com, where he works with business owners, executives, and managers to help them develop the professional relationship skills you've been reading about in this book. He's madly in love with his wife, tries not to spoil his daughter, and will never give up on the New York Knicks. Jonathan is the former CEO and Chief Brand Officer of EMyth, where he led the transformation of a global coaching brand, and has worked in tech, clean tech, and the nonprofit world after graduating law school in 1998. He lives in Ashland, Oregon, a lovely town that's too far away from a warm ocean.